5
conversations
you must have
with your
Daughter

REVISED AND EXPANDED

5 conversations you must have with your Daughter

Vicki Courtney

B&H
PUBLISHING GROUP

NASHVILLE, TENNESSEE

Published by B&H Publishing Group
Nashville, Tennessee

Dewey Decimal Classification: 306.874
Subject Heading: GIRLS \ PARENT AND CHILD \
PARENTING

Cover design by Jennifer Allison of Studio Nth.
Cover photo © 4 PM production / shutterstock.

1 2 3 4 5 6 7 • 23 22 21 20 19

To my daughter, Paige

It has been such a joy to watch you grow into a godly
young woman, wife, and mother. I thank God for the
honor of being not only your mother, but also your friend.

To my granddaughter, Molly

You were so worth the wait! May you grow up
to follow the God of your parents and grandparents
and love Him more than life itself.

Acknowledgments

●　●　●　●　●　●

Keith, as I read through the final manuscript, I was struck with how intentional you have been in discipling our children over the years. Our daughter has been so very blessed to have you for a dad. As long as I live, I will never forget our daughter's rehearsal dinner and you giving her a new locket to hang on the same chain alongside the locket you gave her when she was four years old. Her tears and adoration of you said it all. Every little girl deserves a father like you. What a reward to be on the other side of this parenting journey and see the reward for your faithfulness – the biggest of which is our fast-growing brood of grandchildren!

To my daughter, Paige: When I wrote the original edition of this book, you were wrapping up your senior year of high school and preparing to move over 800 miles from home to attend college. I have to admit that your excitement to leave home left me feeling a bit insecure as I wondered if I'd ever get you back. And yet, here you are today just a few miles away from me! From the day you were born, I dreamed of a day when we would be the best of friends. That day has arrived and not a day goes by that I don't thank God for our relationship. As a bonus, God has given you a daughter and lo and behold if she isn't a carbon copy of your personality at the same age! I bet she may even roll her eyes at you when you attempt some of these conversations in the future, but Mimi has your back! Truly, you are an amazing mother and Molly is blessed to have you in her corner.

To my publisher, B&H: thank you so much for partnering with me to get this message out to moms with daughters.

To the many moms of daughters who encouraged me to write this book and shared your own parenting journeys with me: Thank you so much for your support. Your daughters are blessed to have such caring and concerned mothers.

And last of all, the acknowledgments would not be complete without giving thanks to the one who enables me to write, speak, live, breathe, and love. I pray this book will bring glory and honor to my Savior, Jesus Christ.

Contents

● ● ● ● ● ●

Introduction

When my publisher approached me about updating this book, I eagerly accepted the challenge. Many of the conversations I had presented in the original book had proven relevant to a generation of children growing up in a rapidly changing culture. Never did I imagine that more than 100,000 mothers would pick up a copy of that book. I am humbled beyond belief to play any part in encouraging them in the rearing of their daughters. In the nearly decade that has since passed, new challenges have emerged requiring a tune-up to the original conversations, or in some cases brand new conversations. When I wrote the original book, my oldest son was halfway through college. My daughter was in her senior year of high school and my youngest son was a few years shy of graduating from high school. I was nearing the end of my parenting journey and on the cusp of a new season of life.

In the years that followed my children's launch out of the nest, I guess you could say "the jury was out." I held my breath to see if they would successfully make the transition into adulthood and most importantly, carry their faith with them. There were some bumps along the way, but that was to be expected. And yes, there were times when I wondered if they had paid any attention to the conversations we had along the way, especially when some of their choices indicated otherwise. In those moments, God was faithful to remind me that my ultimate calling was to make "holy deposits" in their lives and trust Him for the results. I adjusted to this new normal where my role as a mother took on a completely different identity. My children needed me every now and then, but overall, they were on their way to becoming independent, self-sufficient young adults. Or so I hoped!

Today, all three of my children are grown adults who are now married and have embarked on their own parenting journeys. They all have a deep faith and are committed to raising their children to know and love God. My empty nest has transitioned into a full nest of half a dozen grandchildren and counting. My husband and I feel extremely blessed that our children live nearby and we see them often. In fact, my daughter only lives a few miles away and hardly a day goes by that I don't see or talk to her. I take great joy in watching her raise her own little mini-me and it's hard not to snicker when she complains about her daughter's stubbornness or strong-will. I love this season of life and wouldn't trade it for anything. I often joke with my friends that "if I'd known how awesome it was to be a grandmother, I would have started with grandkids first."

All this to say, I have enjoyed being somewhat ignorant regarding the challenges facing children today. Updating this book required me to reenter the parenting fray and get back into the trenches, so to speak. In doing so, it didn't take me long to realize that a great deal has changed since the original book released. A whole new generation (iGen or Generation Z) has emerged in place of the Millennials that had been the focus of the previous book. This new generation has some similarities to Millennials, but overall, they are very different. Ironically many of the young parents who will pick up this book (including my own children), are now millennial parents raising iGen or Generation Z children. Essentially, I was faced with the challenge of writing to a brand-new audience of parents raising a brand-new audience of children who are facing a brand-new set of challenges. In an effort to better understand this new generation, I immersed myself into researching what makes them tick. I read countless books and articles focused on iGen or Generation Z children, as well as participated in an online training geared to those who work with this current generation.

Needless to say, I was caught off guard by much of what I discovered related to this emerging generation—record levels of mental illness, depression, loneliness, gender confusion, a lack of identity and purpose, a decreasing interest in marriage and parenthood as future goals, a detachment from the God of the Bible and a rebellion toward His standards and principles, and the list goes on. I would be lying if I told you it didn't take an emotional toll on me at times. My grandchildren are in this generation, so it was personal. I have skin in this game. There were days when I had to take a break from my research and immerse myself in God's Word to be reminded that there is hope. Fortunately, Jesus Christ is the same yesterday, today and forever and none of this has caught Him off guard. His Word never changes and His principles are true for all times. The generation of children today may be growing up in a culture that is resistant to that answer, but that doesn't mean we throw in the towel and give up. God has tasked us with the awesome responsibility to "train up [our] children in the way [they] should go" (Prov. 22:6 ESV), and He never intended that we go it alone.

Ralph Waldo Emerson once said, "It's not the destination, it's the journey." I'm not sure I fully understood that beautiful truth when I wrote the original book. Truth be told, at some level I bought into the naïve belief that if a parent invested enough time and heartache into the rearing of their children, they were guaranteed to arrive safely at the ultimate destination. The problem was, I had the destination all wrong. The destination wasn't an end goal of raising obedient children who have an unblemished track record of devotion to God coupled with a long list of good deeds. Rather, it's about a journey that, much like ours, includes poor choices, many missteps along the way, and hard life lessons that ultimately lead us to a better understanding of God's love, patience, and forgiveness. We are always a work in progress, mothers and daughters alike.

I couldn't be more proud of where my children are today, but I'm not naïve enough to believe it's because I devoted myself to the conversations contained in this book. I've always said there are no foolproof parenting formulas when it comes to raising children. The conversations in this book are simply a tool to better aid you in that journey. Nothing more and nothing less. My children knew that nothing was off limits to talk about—whether they wanted to discuss it or not! The conversations encouraged a healthier pattern of communication that has contributed to the deep friendship I have with each of my children today. For that I am extremely thankful. My children are where they are today because somewhere along the way, they concluded for themselves that the ultimate destination in this journey is a relationship with Jesus Christ. Now, as they are faced with the task of raising their own children, my prayer is that they would set their coordinates on that same destination and point them to Jesus in these uncertain times. He alone is the answer.

And that, my friend, is my prayer for you as well. I won't promise you it will be an easy task. There will be days when you'll want to give up. Fortunately, God never gave up on us! Whatever you do, don't forget to enjoy the journey. It goes by quicker than you think.

Conversation 1

Don't let the culture define you.

Chapter 1

More Than the Sum
of Your Parts

● ● ● ● ● ●

The LORD does not look at the things man looks at. Man looks
at the outward appearance, but the LORD looks at the heart.
(1 Sam. 16:7 NIV, 1984)

Have you ever been lured by pretty packaging? Product manufacturers who aim for successful sales know the importance of packaging. Whether it's a pack of gum, a tube of toothpaste, or a bag of chips, you can bet that countless dollars and hours have been invested into analyzing everything from the target audience to color palettes and shelf placement. The end goal, of course, is for the product to stand out on the shelf and, above all, to get picked up by the consumer and scanned at the checkout.

Now, what if I told you that your little girl is also a product? Her brand managers work around the clock to make sure she knows exactly what it will take to get noticed. If she is to catch the eye of her target audience, the packaging must be perfect. And by *perfect* I mean "flawless." By the time she celebrates her twelfth birthday, she will have seen an estimated 77,546 commercials.[1] Add to it the images she sees daily from magazines, billboards, and the Internet, and you can be certain that by the time she blows out sixteen candles, she will be clear of her role as defined by culture. Over and over again she will be told to lose weight, tone up, dress provocatively, and flaunt it. Pure and simple, she is an object for the male viewing pleasure. She is bidding for male attention among a sea of contenders. And her target audience is picky. He, too, has been inundated with images of picture-perfect women. He has zero tolerance for flat chests, chunky thighs, cellulite, blemishes, split ends, or facial wrinkles. Why should he settle for less than a PhotoShop best? He has come to believe that the airbrushed images are the standard of beauty.

Your daughter has been duped, and it's up to you to expose the lie. If she conforms her identity to the culture's narrow definition of beauty, you can be sure that it will permeate every corner of her life from this moment forward. Ninety-three percent of girls and young women report feeling anxiety or stress about some aspect of their looks when getting ready in the morning. More than three-quarters of girls and young women admit to partaking in unhealthy activities when they feel badly about their bodies. Fifty-eight percent of girls describe themselves in negative terms, including words like *disgusting* and *ugly*, when feeling badly about themselves. Nearly four out of ten engage in unhealthy eating behaviors, such as anorexia or bulimia.[2]

Don't be fooled. Your daughter will be exposed to the lie. Most will fall for it. Some will show outward manifestations when the foundation begins to crack. Others will suffer in silence. They will wear a smile on their face and appear unbothered by the pressure to measure up to this narrow definition of beauty. Their secret will be safe for now. The self-loathing they feel will only be revealed in private when they step out of the shower and catch a glimpse of themselves in the bathroom mirror. Or step on the scales at the doctor's office. Or stand in the department store dressing room as they wrestle into the size they wish they were. Most will never question where this ingrained habit of appearance dissatisfaction took root. It's all they've ever known.

Think about it. How often do you see ad campaigns featuring women that focus on inner beauty? Whether it's advice on fashion, dieting, or pleasing men in the bedroom, the message to our girls is loud and clear. The packaging is of utmost importance. And the reward for a pretty package? A wink perhaps, or a catcall from an onlooker. Some may even be labeled "hot" or "sexy." The grand prize is that the "package" would succeed in becoming the object of the male desire. Isn't that what it's really all about? Ironically, we are almost five decades past the women's movement, and yet women have never been more objectified than they are today.

A Narrow Definition of Beauty

Moms, can you relate to the pressure your daughter feels? I'm betting you can. And trust me, you are not alone. A study commissioned by the Dove Foundation found that 57 percent of all women strongly agree that, "the attributes of female beauty have become very narrowly defined in today's world," and 68 percent strongly agree that "the media and advertising set an unrealistic standard of beauty that most women can't ever achieve."[3]

The challenge to redefine beauty is nothing new. God cautioned His people long ago against judging a person based on the sum of their parts. When Samuel, the prophet, was called by God to anoint the next king to follow Saul, God chastised him for assuming that David's older brother, Eliab, might be next in line to the throne based on his handsome appearance. In 1 Samuel 16:6, Samuel took one look at Eliab and thought, "Surely the LORD's anointed stands here before the LORD." The verse that follows reveals God's standard for judging beauty when He tells Samuel, "Do not consider his appearance or his height, for I have rejected him. The LORD does not look at the things man looks at. People look at the outward appearance, but the LORD looks at the heart" (1 Sam. 16:7).

Together we are going to tackle the culture's lies in order that you might initiate some necessary conversations and arm your daughter with the truth about beauty—God's truth. Whether your daughter has already built a foundation on the culture's lies or is just beginning to be exposed to the brainwashing, trust me, the battle is not lost. Where God is present, there is always hope. Only by speaking up and addressing the lies head-on will we equip our daughters. Our silence, on the other hand, will endorse the culture's lies and leave them with the impression that they amount to nothing more than the sum of their parts. Our daughters need to know that God's standard for beauty is the only standard that matters. Amazingly, His standard used to be the culture's accepted standard. Today we are witnessing the results of a culture that long ago took its eyes off God as the standard for beauty, goodness, and morality.

Vintage Beauty Secrets, Circa 1890

If your daughter were to keep a journal or old-fashioned diary, can you imagine opening it up and reading "Dear Diary, help me to be pretty on the inside." That's what a mother in the late 1800s might be likely to find. Joan Jacobs Brumberg, author of *The Body Project*, researched girls' diaries and journals from the late 1800s to early 1900s to track the shift in attitudes regarding appearance. She found that "before World War I, girls rarely mentioned their bodies in terms of strategies for self-improvement or struggles for personal identity." She stated, "When girls in the nineteenth century thought about ways to improve themselves, they almost always focused on their internal character and how it was reflected in outward behavior. In 1882, the personal agenda of an adolescent diarist read: 'Resolved, not to talk about myself or feelings. To think before speaking. To work seriously. To be self restrained in conversation and actions. Not to let my thoughts wander. To be dignified. Interest myself more in others.'"[4]

Interestingly, Brumberg noted that girls from the nineteenth century were discouraged from showing too much attention to appearance—to do so would be vanity. The book noted that "character was built on attention to self-control, service to others, and belief in God."[5] Young women from the nineteenth century were guided by the wisdom of Proverbs 31:30 that counsels, "Charm is deceptive, and beauty is fleeting; but a woman who fears the LORD is to be praised." Women in the nineteenth century prized virtue over vanity.

Today, one need not go to the trouble of accessing the private diaries and journals of young women to get a pulse on their priorities. They have taken their innermost thoughts and struggles public through social media posts and pictures that would leave their nineteenth-century sisters weeping buckets full of tears. The emphasis on inner beauty has long been forgotten, replaced by a vanity-obsessed selfie generation, desperate for virtual likes and positive comments. A century later the word *virtue* is long forgotten and certainly not part of the average girl's vocabulary. So when and how, exactly, did the shift from virtue to vanity occur? Believe it or not, your bathroom mirror can be partially to blame. In *The Body Project*, Brumberg stated, "When the mirror became a staple of the American middle-class home at the end of the nineteenth century, attention to adolescent acne escalated, as did sales of products for the face. Until then, pimples were primarily a tactile experience, at least for the girl who had them. But that all changed in the late 1800s with the widespread adoption in middle-class homes of a bathroom sink with running water and a mirror hung above it. She further noted that "mirrors play a critical role in the way American girls have assessed their own faces and figures."[6]

As mirrors became popularized, women were able to scrutinize and compare their features with the women they saw in movies and magazines, not to mention one another. In the 1920s, American women began to take an interest in cosmetics. From facial powders to rouge, lipstick, and even eyelash curlers, women flocked to the local drugstores to stock up on these beauty accouterments. The flapper movement further boosted sales of cosmetics among women and especially teenage girls. Blumberg noted that "sales of compacts (small handheld mirrors with a compartment for powder) soared because they allowed women to scrutinize and 'reconstruct' the face almost anywhere, in a moment's notice."[7]

Shortly thereafter, home scales became available, and managing weight became a preoccupation among young women. Until then, the only place a young woman could weigh herself was the drugstore or county fair. Prior to that, dieting and exercise were virtually unheard of, and again, would have been considered a measure of vanity. In fact, I was shocked to discover in Brumberg's book that when young women in the late 1800s left home, they would often write their mothers and speak of healthy weight gain and voracious eating habits. It was almost considered a curse to be slender! Slender girls were thought to be unhealthy and subject to worries of infertility. The ability to bear healthy children was of far greater importance than looking svelte in a swimsuit. As mirrors became more prevalent and the flapper movement gained momentum in the 1920s, women began to express worry over gaining weight, and soon after dieting or "food restriction" became a common topic. The shift from virtue to vanity has been a runaway train ever since.

Mirror, Mirror on the Wall

Stop for a minute and imagine what life might be like without easy access to mirrors and scales. I, for one, stopped weighing myself some years ago in an effort to deconstruct the culture's lie that my happiness is dependent on a certain number on the scale. Having struggled in my teen and college years with an eating disorder, I had cultivated the bad habit of weighing daily, sometimes multiple times within the day. Should the number exceed my defined range of acceptable by even a mere pound, it set the tone of my entire day. Now my focus is on looking healthy rather than stepping on the scale and allowing it to have the final say.

I am certainly not suggesting that we gather up our mirrors and line them up for target practice and toss our scales into the dumpster, but I am questioning the impact they have had on body image among women. Years ago I spoke to a group of young women who were in a sorority at a large university. One of the officers who had invited me had heard my story of misdefined worth in my own college years. She specifically asked that I share about my own experience with an eating disorder as many of the girls living in the sorority house were suffering from eating disorders that ranged from starving themselves to bulimia. In fact, so serious was the issue that they were experiencing plumbing problems due to the pipes prematurely corroding or the toilets stopping up from all the forced vomiting.

When I arrived at the sorority house on the evening I was scheduled to speak, she gave me a quick tour of the house. Along the way I couldn't help but notice that there were mirrors everywhere. Entire walls had been turned into mirrors in the large meeting room and in the living area. In addition, full-length mirrors were staggered up and down the hallways and along the grand stairwell. When I made a comment about the mirrors being everywhere, she quickly replied, "Why do you think so many of our girls are starving themselves and throwing up? The mirrors serve as a constant reminder that they can never measure up." At that moment I longed for the mirrorless days of the late 1800s, a time when virtue was considered beauty and vanity was considered sin. While it might not be possible to do away with mirrors, it is possible to do away with some of the expectations women have when they see their reflections in the mirrors.

Geometry 101

Few girls are prepared for the stage when they transition from little girls to young women and their bodies began to develop almost at warp speed. As if it's not enough to manage the influx of hormones and the start of the menstrual cycle, they must also make peace with their bodies as they begin to take on a more womanly shape. This should be one of the most celebrated times of life for all that it symbolizes, but sadly, that is not the case for most girls. One survey found that by age thirteen, 53 percent of American girls are unhappy with their bodies, and by age seventeen 78 percent are dissatisfied.[8] If we are to counter the culture's lies regarding body image, we must first go to the root of the problem and address body shape. I am talking about the God-given body shape your daughter was born with rather than the hourglass ideal the media insists she should have. Amazingly, a study found that the hourglass figure is the least dominant shape of women, having made up only 8 percent of the 6,318 U.S. women that were scanned for the study.[9] Keep in mind that the average woman is 5 feet 3.7 inches and weighs 168.5 pounds.[10] The same study found that the garment industry assumes that the hourglass figure is the dominant shape of American women and designs their clothing accordingly. Because of this misconception, many women are unable to find clothes designed to flatter their body shape, and as a result, they struggle to make peace with their God-given body shape. In fact, 46 percent of women were found to have more of a rectangular shape, 21 percent were spoon shaped, and 14 percent were shaped more like an inverted triangle.[11]

Putting the geometry lesson aside, imagine a world where there were no manufactured sizes. A world used to exist over a century ago when clothing was made at home. In *The Body Project*, Blumberg noted, "In general, mass-produced clothing fostered autonomy in girls because it took matters of style and taste outside the dominion of the mother, who had traditionally made and supervised a girl's wardrobe. . . . So long as clothing was made at home, the dimensions of the garment could be adjusted to the particular body intended to wear it. But with store-bought clothes, the body had to fit instantaneously into standard sizes that were constructed from a pattern representing a norm. When clothing failed to fit the body, particularly a part as intimate as the breasts, young women were apt to perceive that there was something wrong with their bodies."[12]

I doubt many of us are willing to retreat back to the days where mothers sewed their children's clothes (nor would our daughters allow it!). However, knowing the history and time line of manufactured sizes reminds us that a time existed when allowances were made for unique shapes and sizes without the pressures many women feel today to fit into a certain size. Not to mention, they were less likely to compare themselves to others since they didn't think of their bodies in terms of a certain size.

The Weight Debate

A published report by Common Sense Media found that more than half of girls as young as six to eight feel their ideal body is thinner than their current body size.[13] Young girls say that they are more afraid of becoming fat than they are of cancer, nuclear war, or losing their parents.[14] Additionally, a survey by the Today Show and AOL.com in 2014 found that "80 percent of teen girls compare themselves to images they see of celebrities, and, within that group, almost half say the images make them feel dissatisfied with the way they look."[15] Approximately 50 percent of teenage girls will engage in unhealthy weight control behaviors.[16]

However, there is also a flip side. The number of overweight adolescents in the U.S. has tripled since 1970s. Data from 2015–2016 show that nearly one in five school-age children and young people (six to nineteen years) in the United States has obesity.[17] It certainly doesn't help that the average child is exposed to more than forty thousand television ads a year, and the majority are for food products and target young people. Add to this the decrease in physical activity, and we have a major problem.[18]

What exactly is the balance when talking to our daughters about dieting and nutrition? On the one hand, we want them to steer clear of eating disorders, but on the other, we don't want them to experience the dangers of being overweight. It's a tricky balance. Our goal should be to educate our girls to the dangers of both extremes. Our emphasis should not be placed on achieving a target weight range but rather on developing healthy eating habits and exercising on a regular basis. Which begs the question: Is a healthy diet really a diet? No! When we stop looking at these diet plans (eating the foods that are good for us in smaller, more reasonable quantities) as quick fixes and start viewing them as a way of life, we win, and our daughters win. Here's the way I see it: We can talk to our daughters about the dangers of eating disorders and/or being overweight, or we can both talk *and* act. In doing so, you provide a solution by defeating both extremes, and you increase the odds that they will carry their healthy habits into their adult years.

Below are a few tips to help your daughter have a positive body image:

1. Give your daughter positive messages that she is beautiful and attractive. In *Teenage Girls: Exploring Issues Adolescent Girls Face and Strategies to Help Them,* author Ginny Olson states that "mothers especially have a clear impact on their daughter's body image. Girls who have strong and healthy relationships with their mothers are more likely to have a higher sense of self-confidence and a lower incidence of eating disorders."[19]

2. Watch what you say about your own bodies! Darlene Atkins, the director of the Eating Disorders Clinic at Children's National Medical Center in Washington states, "Sadly, mothers especially are often very critical of their own weight and shape, and their girls absorb that."[20]

3. Make the focus in your home nutrition rather than weight loss. In the article, "For Teens, Obesity No Laughing Matter," Atkins advocated making home into a "safe zone," primarily by emphasizing feeding one's body in a healthy way, so that it functions at a healthy level—not by dwelling on restrictive dieting. To further support the need to back up our talk with action, Kay Abrams, a clinical psychologist and eating disorders expert, says, "Live by your actions and your lifestyle. Don't lecture and talk about weight all the time. Just change."[21]

4. Never tease your daughter about her weight. According to new research from the University of Minnesota, teasing adolescents about weight—especially if the teasing comes from family members—can play a big role in future weight problems. The study found that girls who were teased about their weight were about twice as likely to be overweight five years later as other girls who weren't. In addition, they were also about 1.5 times more likely to engage in binge eating and use extreme weight-control behaviors, like purging or abuse of laxatives, diuretics, or diet pills. Even more disturbing, the study found that almost half of the overweight girls surveyed were teased by their families, compared to 34 percent of overweight boys. Note that this is not teasing as in harassment but rather simple statements made tongue-in-cheek: "Are you sure you should eat that?" or "Whoa there! That milk shake will go straight to your thighs!"[22]

The Truth about Aging

Time, wrote John Milton, is "the subtle thief of youth." Perhaps there is no more painful reminder of that truth than a torturous afternoon spent trying to find the perfect swimsuit to flatter a post-fifty shape. Did I say flatter? I meant HIDE! See, there I go, exposing my own susceptibility to the media's lie that fifty is the new thirty. Give me a break.

Recently the popular Dove Campaign for Real Beauty sought to expose the general public to a more realistic picture of aging when they released pictures in an ad campaign of older women in the equivalent of their undergarments. They were untouched images that exposed the reality of the natural aging process. They were healthy-sized women with curves, dimples, cellulite, and age spots. While there was controversy over the ads being too racy to be in magazines, part of me was glad to see at least an attempt (though radical) to expose the media's anti-aging obsession.

Whether it's images of women in ad campaigns or on magazine covers, the trend of airbrushing every well-earned wrinkle and laugh-line has left our young women with unrealistic expectations regarding the aging process. In *The Beauty Myth: How Images of Beauty Are Used against Women*, author Naomi Wolf said,

"Magazines, consciously or half-consciously, must project the attitude that looking one's age is bad because $650 million of their ad revenue comes from people who would go out of business if visible age looked good."[23]

How do we even begin to tackle this topic with our daughters and give them a more realistic picture of the natural aging process? How can we convince them that "gray hair is a crown of splendor" (Prov. 16:31) when many of us, myself included, are rushing to our hairdressers and paying them to cover it up, one gray hair at a time? Ouch! I for one am not feeling so led to give up my highlights, occasional manicures, and magical eye cream, so it's important to find a balance. Are you at peace, for the most part, with the aging process, or are you kicking and screaming about every gray hair and facial wrinkle?

I recently stumbled upon some interesting information regarding the aging process. If you're young, read it and weep. If you're old and your kids are kind enough to remind you on a daily basis, read it and weep and then torment your kids with the information! According to an article on CNN.com, there are six stages of life: infancy, childhood, adolescence, young adulthood, middle adulthood, and senior adulthood.

The description of young adulthood is what caught me by surprise. Here is what it says: "A person reaches physical maturity and stops growing around age eighteen. As early as age twenty, people may notice the beginning signs of aging; fine wrinkles, thinning skin, loss of firmness in hands and neck, graying hair, hair loss and thinning nails. At age thirty, the human body's major organs begin to decline."[24]

The next time your kids heckle you about being old, smile and say, "Well, your turn is coming, and it may be sooner than you think." I then seized the opportunity to inform them that their bodies may show signs of aging in their twenties and their organs will begin shutting down around thirty. Okay, so maybe "shutting down" is a bit harsh, but you get my point.

We need to make sure our daughters realize that the images they are seeing in the media of models and celebrities who appear to have found the fountain of youth are not real. Most have been prepped for the photo session by hair and makeup artists, Botox, plastic surgery, and even after all that, will likely be airbrushed beyond recognition. We need to set a positive example for our daughters and make friends with the aging process. That doesn't mean we have to let our hair go gray and wear it in a tight bun atop our heads and fill our closets with holiday sweaters and Naturalizer footwear. I for one enjoy dressing fashionably, getting my hair highlighted, and treating myself to an occasional spa service.

There is nothing wrong with beautifying the temple as long as it's done in good taste and is not your primary focus. If our daughters are constantly subjected to our grumblings as we journey through the aging process, it will leave them with the impression that life is somehow less appealing in the latter years. Let's quit this nonsense of being shocked and surprised when our bodies begin to show some wear and tear.

Beauty Redefined

After discussing in depth the lies both we and our daughters have been told regarding the narrow definition of beauty, we are left with the task of redefining beauty. Only then can we pass along a healthy definition to our daughters. Sadly, only 4 percent of women would describe themselves as beautiful.[25] Are you in that small sampling? Is your daughter in that small sampling?

What exactly is beauty? The Dove Campaign asked women and found that:

- Thirty-two percent of women say their biggest beauty pressure is the one they put on themselves.
- Seven out of ten women agree that beauty is more than physical appearance.
- Eighty-eight percent state that every woman has something about her that is beautiful.[26]

Now, stop for a minute and think about it. When you hear (or say) the phrase, "She is beautiful," is it made in reference to what is on the outside or the inside? I find it sad that popular culture and the mass media have hijacked the authentic definition of beauty. Beauty is defined by God and God alone. He sets the standard for beauty and gives us clues throughout Scripture as to what defines a beautiful woman. Unfortunately, the secular definition of beauty given by women in the Dove survey failed to recognize the key component that determines a woman's happiness, confidence, dignity, and humor. That key component, of course, is faith. Just as the Proverbs 31 passage concludes, "Charm is deceptive, and beauty is fleeting; but a woman who fears the LORD is to be praised" (Prov. 31:30). Faith in a loving and forgiving God will be the root of any and all manifestations of beauty. Physical beauty will fade over time, but true beauty (virtue) is timeless.

Damage Control

As parents, that's where we come in. Only by pointing out the lies of culture and continually reminding our daughters of God's definition of beauty and sexuality will we stand a chance of protecting our daughters from the culture's inevitable brainwashing. We must be faithful in reminding them that beauty is not defined by a number on the scale, a manufactured clothing size, an hourglass shape, washboard abs, slender thighs, big boobs, pouty bee-stung lips, a pair of designer jeans, a cleavage-baring top, a new sassy haircut, a clear complexion, the latest and greatest anti-wrinkle cream, or a surgical procedure. While some of the above may temporarily boost self-esteem or garner attention from men, they don't impress God in the least.

If we are to engage successfully in the worthy conversation, "You are more than the sum of your parts" with our daughters, we must first do a self-check and make sure we believe it ourselves. For those of us who have been thoroughly brainwashed by the culture over the years, this will be a difficult challenge. And, I dare say, that would likely be the majority of women reading this book! While I hope that this book will help you better engage in the necessary and ongoing conversation with your daughters regarding body image and appearance, I pray that the truths presented will aid you in breaking free from the culture's lies.

In a world that beckons our daughters to grow up far too fast, it's never too soon to begin the conversation with our daughters regarding true beauty in the eyes of God. In the appendix, I have included a list of key Scriptures related to appearance and beauty. Some are verses I have referenced in preceding chapters, but they bear repeating! Wouldn't it be nice if our girls grew up with these verses tucked away in their hearts? I have also included some tips for combatting the narrow definition of beauty based on the age of your daughter. I encourage you to take a look at the verses and talking points and go over them with your daughters. God has given us the definition of true beauty and it's up to us to make sure our daughters see themselves through His eyes rather than the eyes of the world.

Chapter 2

Girlhood Interrupted

●　●　●　●　●　●

For everything there is a season, and a time for
every matter under heaven. (Eccles. 3:1 ESV)

Just recently I was going through some old photographs and
stumbled upon a heartwarming picture of my daughter and four
of her friends at the tender age of nine. They were standing side by
side and proudly posing, each one cradling her respective American
Girl doll. I remembered taking the picture, their innocent smiles
reflective of what being a "tween" girl is all about. I recall wondering, at the time, how much longer they would be content with
dressing up their dolls and throwing them pretend birthday parties.

A couple of months after taking that photo, one of the same
girls in the picture came over to spend the night and left her doll
behind at home. Instead, she brought over a newly purchased CD.
The mock birthday parties they used to stage with their dolls
were replaced on this evening with a late-night concert, starring of

course, my daughter and her friend. With the boom box blaring at top volume and their karaoke mics in hand, they were belting out the chorus of a new song, "Hit Me Baby One More Time," by an up-and-coming artist, Britney Spears. I wasn't familiar with this artist at the time, but she looked to be a mere child herself, posing innocently on the front of the CD cover with her hands in a prayer-like stance.

As I watched my daughter and her friend sing into their mics like little pop stars, it hit me at that moment that a battle was looming on the distant horizon—a battle, mind you, that would pit a concerned mom against a culture bent on robbing her daughter of her girlhood. How ironic that less than a decade later the pop star on that CD cover would become the poster child for all that can go wrong when you grow up at warp speed.

That day I only saw my own little girl and her friend standing on the banks and dipping their big toe in the water. The current was slow moving; and, though they appeared somewhat curious about what lay beyond, their feet were still firmly planted on the bank. Two years later, at the age of twelve, she would make the dreaded request to put her dolls away. Up until that point her dolls were a permanent fixture in her room, as much a part of the decor as the lime green velvet curtains and the fuzzy beanbag chair in the corner.

"Are you sure?" I asked, hopeful she would change her mind. "What if one of your friends comes over and wants to bring her doll?"

Without hesitation, she confidently declared, "Mom, we're twelve now. That's not going to happen."

I don't know what stung my heart more: the signal that the doll phase was over and out or the reminder that she was, in fact, twelve and one year shy of officially being a teen. And so I began the difficult task of neatly packing away her dolls, doll clothes, and doll furniture in sturdy, plastic storage bins—sensing at the time that it signaled the close of one chapter and the beginning of another. I tried desperately to stifle my tears as I shoved the bins onto the top shelf in her closet. I reasoned that their new home was far superior to the hot, stuffy attic and much more convenient should my daughter change her mind and decide to release her dolls from their plastic prison. In my heart I knew the top shelf would likely remain their permanent home.

Packing her dolls away was minor in comparison to packing her belongings and moving her into a dorm more than eight hundred miles from home six years later. Where did the time go? It seems like she hardly noticed the transition from little girl to tween, tween to teen, and teen to young woman. Oh, but I did. And I did my best to make sure she relished each and every season. Proudly, my daughter was ten going on ten, sixteen going on sixteen, eighteen going on eighteen, and transitioned confidently into young womanhood. A good majority of girls her age left the shallow banks of girlhood far too soon and were swept along by the fast-moving currents of the culture. And unfortunately, many had bumps and bruises to show for the journey.

Many of you reading this find yourself where I was when I was packing away the dolls. One day your daughter is very much a little girl, and the next day she is showing signs of restlessness. Others of you perhaps are breathing a huge sigh of relief that you're not there yet. Enjoy the days you have, and don't rush your little girl to grow up. Fight for every moment of her girlhood, and don't allow the culture to get its foot in the door. Perhaps others are reading this, and your daughters are being swept away in the current. You desperately want to throw them a lifeline, but you're not even certain they would reach for it. You may be thinking, *Too little, too late.* No! Don't give up that easy. In fact, let me give you this hope: You are the great and mighty gatekeeper when it comes to providing your daughter with a much-needed umbrella of protection. In other words, you have the power to say "yes," "no," or "wait" when these influences come knocking. If you haven't set parameters in advance, it won't be easy, but it's not impossible.

If I had to pinpoint one common denominator that is commonly shared among girls who grow up too fast, it would be this: a set of parents or a parent who, for whatever reasons, stood by on the shoreline and allowed their daughter to wander in too deep. Many, I dare say, even cheered their girls on as if there was some sort of prize at the finish line. What type of parent would allow this to happen? Below, I will describe four styles of parenting that create the perfect storm for raising a daughter who can be on the fast track to growing up.

Dangerous Parenting Styles

"Buddy-buddy" Parents. There is nothing wrong with being your child's friend as long as you are the parent first. These "buddy-buddy" parents are more focused on being their child's friend than their parent, and will often attempt to avoid conflict in an effort to stay in favor with their child. Buddy-buddy parents are lax on boundaries and prone to giving into requests made by their child. A root cause of buddy-buddy parenting is low self-esteem. Being viewed as "cool" by their child and their child's friends can be a boost to esteem. Ironically, the child is rarely sincere about the friendship and plays along to manipulate the results. Additionally,

the parent's true motive in seeking to be best buds is not really done for the goal of prioritizing the child; rather it's about the parents' need for approval.

Even if you do not embrace this parenting style, you need to be aware that there are many parents who do. When my daughter was in high school, I was tipped off by a concerned parent to some disturbing photos on social media of a party that took place at the home of a student from my daughter's high school. Fortunately, my daughter was not in attendance at this party where alcohol was flowing freely from a keg in the garage and the kitchen counter was littered with beer cans.

As I looked at the pictures that were so brazenly posted online, I had to wonder, *Where in the world are the parents?* Minutes later, I found my answer: a picture of good ol' dad in the kitchen posing with some of the girls, each of them with a beer in hand. And another picture of dad's girlfriend posing in between two high school guys who appear to be holding her up. By the looks of the picture, I suspect she's filled up her cup one too many times at the keg she and good ol' dad probably purchased. I even found another picture of dad's girlfriend "booty-dancing" with one of the girls in the kitchen. I don't know this couple, but I couldn't help but wonder if the parents of the other kids at the party (or the police, for that matter) would think they're cool for supplying alcohol to minors. Do they not realize that they are partially to blame if one person leaves that party intoxicated and an accident occurs? While this is an extreme example of parents who are more interested in being their child's friend than parent, this style of parenting is on the rise.

"Too Busy to Care" Parents. These are typically the parents who are running themselves ragged in their jobs or activities and left with little time to be engaged when it comes to parenting their child. Parenting is hard work and takes tremendous amounts of time and energy to stay engaged in what is going on in their child's life. Drawing up boundaries, maintaining the boundaries, and address-ing issues when the boundary lines are crossed take time. If time is short, these parents put aside parenting and only address critical issues as they arise, often reacting only after the damage has been done. In a culture that esteems constant busyness, many parents have accepted that busyness is the norm pace and as a result, are left with little to no margin to invest in the training and protection of their children. Even if you have not embraced this parenting style, you can expect that many of your children's friends' parents have.

"Too Tuned Out to Notice" Parents. These are typically the parents whose temperaments lend themselves to a more laid-back parenting style. While being laid-back can be a positive quality in parenting, it can also be a detriment if it results in few boundaries and little, if any, boundary enforcement. Again, because parenting requires round-the-clock diligence and an ability to stay engaged in the issues impacting our children, "too tuned out to notice" parents often fail to see what's going on around them. These parents are the most likely to extend too much benefit-of-the-doubt to their kids and say things like, "Kids will be kids," or, "What I don't know won't hurt me." Ignorance is not always bliss and oftentimes, it leads to more work on the backend when tuned-out parents are left to sweep up the mess in the aftermath of lax boundaries and little to no supervision. Too much is at stake to check out and let your children raise themselves.

"Living through My Kid to Feel Better about Myself" Parents. Oh boy, if you haven't seen these parents in action, head to the nearest ball field/cheer gym/booster club meeting for a sighting.

The root of this type of parenting is usually low self-esteem and a need to please/impress others. "Look at my child! He/she is popular/athletic/smart/attractive" you-fill-in-the-blank; and therefore, that makes the parent feel *important*. Another end result of this type of parenting is an unhealthy concentration on "image maintenance." These are typically the parents who make sure their child looks good and performs well at all times since they typically see their children as reflections of themselves unless, of course, the children fail and then we have a problem. If children succeed, parents feel like they succeed. And if children fail, parents take it personally and blame the child/coach/teacher or whoever is nearby to point blame. Therefore, failure is not an option.

Truth be told, many of us (myself included) may lapse into one or more of the parenting styles above from time to time. Only by looking to God for strength and wisdom when it comes to parenting our children will we find the proper balance needed. Who among us is really prepared when our sweet little angels are begging to go to Build-a-Bear one day, and get a padded bra the next? Or they ask for a smartphone because they are "the only one who doesn't have one in their grade"? Or they jump into the social media cesspool before you've had time to figure out if they're ready? Or they want to buy those short-shorts and barely-there tops? Or they get tagged in a group picture online where they are posing provocatively? What will you say? Most importantly, are you prepared to say "no" if it would expose her to influences that would rush her to grow up too soon? Even if most of her friends' parents are saying "yes"? Engaged, intentional parents care more about pleasing God than gaining favor with their child. Managing the milestones will require diligent attention to the influences that intersect her path. Do you have a battle plan when it comes to key interrupters that threaten to rob your daughter of her girlhood? If you don't have a current battle plan, or you hadn't thought much about it until now, let me encourage you to review the key interrupters below and begin to develop one. Talk openly with your daughter about these influencers, so she will better understand your position and the reason behind your rules. And you might want to rehearse this line over and over again because you're going to be saying it often: "That might be okay in _____'s house, but it's not okay in ours."

Key Interrupters

Extracurricular Over-commitment

If I could go back and have a little chat with my younger mom self, one of the first things I'd tell her is to lighten up on the extracurricular madness that has become the norm for most families. I bought into the lie that the key to raising happy, healthy children was to expose them to a multitude of activities in their growing up years. How else would you help them discover their unique gifts and talents? If I could go back and do the parenting thing all over again, I would sign my kids up for less activities (especially in the younger years) and build more time into the schedule for free time.

Somewhere along the way, we got the idea that it is a bad thing for children to have down time or actually be *bored*. Some of my greatest childhood memories were of times when I had to figure out ways to fill the empty blocks in my day. I have fond memories of playing kickball in the cul-de-sac of my neighborhood, collecting rocks, and even simple pleasures like playing in the rain. I was part of the generation that grew up experiencing the great outdoors. Every day was a new adventure. Whether it was a game of tag, hide-and-seek, or a game of add-on on the neighbor's trampoline, we created our own fun. Sadly, you no longer see children playing outdoors in many suburban neighborhoods, partially because their schedules have been micro-managed from morning to night. Children today are stressed out like never before and we wonder why. Our daughters will never get another opportunity to enjoy their childhood. Why rush them through it by endorsing a pace that most adults couldn't sustain?

Excessive Screen-time

We will cover the topic of technology more extensively in Conversation 2, but it is necessary to mention it here, since it will likely be the greatest threat you face when it comes to protecting your daughter's girlhood. As more and more evidence emerges related to the impact of screen time usage and mental health among adolescents, this will be a battle worth fighting. And battle, it will be, since kids are being handed smartphones at younger and younger ages. I know it's time-consuming, but monitor your daughter's activity anytime she goes online. Take advantage of parental controls and monitoring software that can alert you to their activity.

Most importantly, don't allow your daughter to engage in any form of unmonitored online activity before she is emotionally ready to disseminate what she sees. (This age will vary from girl to girl, but it's safe to say a grade-schooler or middle-schooler is not equipped to carry the emotional burden that comes with too much screen-time and especially, social media.) Their brains are only half-baked at this point and excessive screen-time and/or exposure to mature themes can literally rewire their brains and affect their mental health. Some girls will be at risk of addiction, especially if addiction runs in the family. I realize this may sound alarmist in nature, but the evidence is beginning to stack up related to the fall-out of allowing too much screen time.

Smartphones

As the first generation that are true tech natives, your children are in essence, guinea pigs to this electronic social experiment. Sure, technology and screens are here to stay, but don't be fooled into believing the lie that it's necessary to introduce it early for fear your child will later be behind or at a disadvantage. Our children will be quick adapters whether they are handed a device at five or fifteen. On the flipside, they will never get another shot at being a kid. Postpone smartphones for as long as possible. If you want them to have a phone for safety reasons, give them one with limited features until they are ready to handle the responsibility that comes with a smartphone and unlimited access. Once you decide to get them a smartphone, I would recommend investing in one of the mobile software monitoring apps or services. Most will come with a monthly charge, but view it as an investment into your daughter's future mental health.

Social Media

Several years ago, I received an email from a concerned mother and pastor's wife who had recently discovered her twelve-year-old daughter was cutting. The discovery came as a complete shock to the mother who said it was out of character for her daughter to engage in such a risky behavior. She was a straight-A student and involved in extracurricular activities. In addition to having two loving, and engaged parents in the home, she also had many close friends and was involved in her church youth group. The mother went on to share that after several counseling sessions, the root of the problem had been discovered. They had recently allowed their daughter to engage in a popular social media app with some time limitations and protective boundaries in place. She was required to keep her account private and give her mother her login information, so her mother could monitor her activity from time to time. Even so, the mother didn't notice any unusual activity that might have triggered her daughter's cutting.

And that was the problem. There were no comments that implied bullying. Nor was there any contact from a stranger making inappropriate requests. Her daughter confessed to the counselor that she began cutting herself because she felt worthless when she compared herself to everyone else's highlight reel. The triggers weren't obvious, but at the same time, they were out in the open for all to see. Her daughter struggled to understand why some of her friends' pictures got more likes than her pictures. Or why some of the girls she thought were her friends didn't follow her back. She was stressed over pictures of girls who she perceived to be prettier and more fashionable, and had the comments and likes from the popular boys to prove it. Or the pictures of some of her friends hanging out together—without her. She began to obsess over perfectly timed posts with witty status updates that might garner her more likes and followers, but it never seemed to be enough. The more time she spent on the app, the more she felt she could never measure up.

Social media can take a toll on your soul, regardless of age. Most of the sites require a minimum age to participate, but a parent should not let that be their barometer. Many girls are not emotionally mature enough to handle the pressures and stress associated with social media until they are in their mid to late teens. Even then, it may be too much for some girls who are prone to comparison, low self-image, being bullied or bullying others, and other issues that are often magnified on social media. I've mentioned this already, but I would highly recommend that you not allow your daughter to engage in social media apps unless you also invest in monitoring software to track her usage in an effort to protect her mental health. Great strides have been made in monitoring software for mobile devices and some are able to track activity on the popular social media apps where teens often trade pictures and videos that have a time stamp. (In the appendix, I offer some links to monitoring software that may be beneficial to parents.)

Media with Hyper-sexualized or Adult Themes

Years ago, the American Psychological Association issued a warning after a task force studied the proliferation of sexualized images of girls and young women in advertising, merchandising, and media. Not surprisingly, they found the images are harmful to girls' self-image and healthy development.[1] Every forum of media was fair game, including video games, song lyrics, magazines, and the round-the-clock bombardment of sexual images found on television and the Internet.

Sexualization was defined by the task force as occurring when a person's value comes only from her/his sexual appeal or behavior, to the exclusion of other characteristics, and when a person is sexually objectified, i.e., made into a thing for another's sexual use. While the overall finding of the study may not come as a surprise, it should serve as a wake-up call for parents who have somehow rationalized that it's a battle not worth fighting. Take a look at some of the fall-out the study confirmed:

- Cognitive and Emotional Consequences: Sexualization and objectification undermine a person's confidence in and comfort with her own body, leading to emotional and self-image problems such as shame and anxiety.

- Mental and Physical Health: Research links sexualization with three of the most common mental health problems diagnosed in girls and women—eating disorders, low self-esteem, and depression or depressed mood.
- Sexual Development: Research suggests that the sexualization of girls has negative consequences on girls' ability to develop a healthy sexual self-image.[2]

According to the task force report, parents can play a major role in contributing to the sexualization of their daughters, or they can play a protective and educational role. The study acknowledges that parents may actually contribute to the sexualization of their daughters in a number of ways.

In the book *Teenage Girls: Exploring Issues Adolescent Girls Face and Strategies to Help Them,* author Ginny Olson states:

Early adolescent girls are especially vulnerable to media images. They're constantly searching for information to guide them as to how they should look and behave in this new world. As concrete thinkers, they haven't yet developed the necessary skills for discerning the different messages the media is sending. It's not until they reach about middle adolescence that they begin to develop the ability to scrutinize media messages and evaluate the themes with a certain level of skepticism. By the time they reach seventeen or eighteen, they've had enough experience with the media to be able to assess and reject the messages.[3]

As our daughters get older, it's nearly impossible to monitor every TV show and movie they may watch or stream on a device, not to mention every website they might visit, but it would go a long way to ban movies and block shows/cable channels/websites and the like that are known for being sexually provocative or explicit in nature. Additionally, sit in and listen to the shows your kids are watching to ensure they are appropriate, and take advantage of sites that review TV series and movies before allowing your children to watch them. Also, the Parents Television Council (www.parentstv.org) rates the most popular shows among kids and compiles a "best and worst shows" list based on the content. They also have a fabulous feature where you can select a popular show and read the corresponding review.

When it comes to objectionable shows or websites like YouTube where they might easily stumble upon objectionable material, I highly recommend that parents install web filters and monitoring software to add as many layers of protection as possible. It will be impossible to protect them 100 percent of the time; and as they get older, they can access these channels/shows at friends' houses. This is why it is of utmost importance that parents take advantage of teachable moments and carefully explain the why behind your rules.

Sexualized Fashion

As parents we must help our daughters realize that their clothing is like a label. When they wear skin-baring fashions, it often sends a message to others about their character. The APA study that I cited previously had this to say:

> If girls purchase (or ask their parents to purchase) products and clothes designed to make them look physically

appealing and sexy, and if they style their identities after the sexy celebrities who populate their cultural landscape, they are, in effect, sexualizing themselves. Girls also sexualize themselves when they think of themselves in objectified terms. Psychological researchers have identified self-objectification as a key process whereby girls learn to think of and treat their own bodies as objects of others' desires. In self-objectification, girls internalize an observer's perspective on their physical selves and learn to treat themselves as objects to be looked at and evaluated for their appearance.[4]

Let me break that powerful statement down for you. When we (parents) allow our daughters to dress in a revealing manner, we play a part in sexualizing and objectifying them. Not to mention, many girls are not yet able to make a connection between what they wear and the reaction it may generate among the opposite sex. The APA study found that "girls are experiencing teen pressures at younger and younger ages. However, they are not able to deal with these issues because their cognitive development is out of sync with their social, emotional and sexual development. Let girls be girls."

It is up to us to have this necessary conversation (over and over again) with our daughters and remind them that clothing sends a strong message; and it may, in fact, be a message that misrepresents who they really are. When it comes to sporting the perfect outfit, we need to let our daughters know that there is nothing wrong with dressing fashionably as long as it meets God's standard of dress— "modestly, with decency, and propriety" (1 Tim. 2:9).

When it comes to the temptation to grow up too fast, I am reminded of the description of Susan in C. S. Lewis's classic Narnia book, *The Last Battle*:

"She's interested in nothing nowadays except nylons and lipstick and invitations. She always was a jolly sight too keen on being grown-up."

"Grown-up, indeed," said the Lady Polly. "I wish she would grow up. She wasted all her school time wanting to be the age she is now, and she'll waste all the rest of her life trying to stay that age. Her whole idea is to race on to the silliest time of one's life as quick as she can and then stop there as long as she can."[5]

Girlhood will last only for a brief season and, once gone, can never be revisited. Why rush this precious time? It's up to us to help our daughters enjoy the ages they are now rather than the ages they may wish to be. Youthful innocence—once gone—can never be retrieved.

Chapter 3

Identity Crisis

● ● ● ● ● ●

I praise you because I am fearfully and wonderfully made;
your works are wonderful, I know that full well. (Ps. 139:14)

While recently thumbing through a sales catalog advertising a line of teen furnishings, I ran across a particular image that included several teen models. A girl was sitting on a furry, neon-colored beanbag chair. Standing within a few feet of her was a guy, smiling and gesticulating as though engaged in conversation. And next to him was another guy. Or wait, was it a girl? The model had short hair and wore skinny jeans and a baggy button shirt. He/she was lanky with androgynous facial features that appeared neither overtly masculine nor feminine. I looked for any hint that might tip the scale in one direction, but I finally gave up.

Since stumbling upon that ad with the androgynous model, Bruce Jenner has had elective surgery to become Caitlin Jenner, Covergirl named a seventeen-year-old boy to be the face for their

2017 campaign, and Facebook announced it would be expanding its gender identification options to include over fifty choices. Should a user not be able to find an option that suits them, they also offer an additional option to self-identify.

As we stray further and further from a biblical model of manhood and womanhood, our daughters (and sons) will grow up in a world where gender-fluid is the new norm. *Gender-fluid* can be defined as "noting or relating to a person whose gender identity or gender expression is not fixed and shifts over time or depending on the situation."[1] A recent survey, 69 percent of teens (age thirteen to eighteen) said it is acceptable to "be born one gender and feel like another." Thirty-three percent of teens surveyed said gender is primarily based on "what a person feels like." Three in ten teens surveyed reported personally knowing someone, most often a peer, who has changed his or her identity. One in eight teens (12 percent) describe their sexual orientation as something other than heterosexual or straight.[2] Compare this to the approximate 3 percent of adults who have identified with being LGBT. Why is this important? The current generation of teens (iGen/Generation Z)—more than any other generation before them—considers their sexuality or gender to be central to their sense of personal identity.[3]

If we are to raise daughters who are confident in their womanhood, and thus, their core identity, we must be aware of the outside influences that seek to undermine God's design for gender and sexuality. Genesis 1:27 reminds us that God created man in His own image. "Male and female He created them." Men and women are different because God created them to be distinctly different. There are no allowances in the passage for additional genders or for that matter, non-genders. It is the natural order set in motion by our creator God and anything that suggests otherwise is a deviation from that natural order. Our daughters are growing up in a day when such views are considered narrow-minded and bigoted. The gender-fluid movement has gained traction and like it or not, our daughters will be exposed to this increasingly accepted deviation from God's natural order.

Lest you think this movement is not gaining traction, consider that this past year, a mother at an event where I was the speaker shared that her daughter was given in-school detention for "incorrectly stating there are only two genders." As part of her suspension, she was required to memorize a list of politically correct gender pronouns created by the school in an effort to respect the broad list of identities represented among the student body. I thought I'd heard it all when the mother added that one girl in her daughter's class has shared that she identifies as "feline." While my initial reaction to hearing her account was one of shock and even outrage that Christians would be forced to abide by a policy that enforces the ridiculous assumption that a person can identify with being anything they want to be (including a cat), my anger quickly turned to compassion. How sad that so many of our children and youth are desperately searching for identity and purpose and our culture has led them down a path that will leave them even more confused and empty in the end.

As mothers, our goal should be to teach our children the tedious balance of walking in Truth and leading with love. We need to be intentional when it comes to making sure our daughters understand the creation account and God's design for womanhood and likewise, manhood. However, we must also teach our children to be kind and compassionate to others who don't share their same values and beliefs. Romans 3:23 reminds us, "for all have sinned and fall short of the glory of God." Rarely, do we win converts to Christianity by being combative and loudly pointing out how others fall short of God's standards.

Jesus illustrated this balance throughout His earthly ministry when He encountered those who were in sin. His end goal was not to implement a moral code of behavior, but rather, to change hearts. When He encountered the Samaritan woman at a well (John 4), He didn't chastise her for having had five husbands in the past and living at the time with a man who wasn't her husband. His focus was on her true need rather than her deeds. He loved her enough to meet with her one-on-one and engage in a conversation in order that He might offer her living water (forgiveness of sin).

Our daughters are growing up in a world where it's not uncommon for self-proclaiming Christians to compromise Truth in effort to bend to the customs of an ever-changing culture. It's up to us to make sure our daughters understand God's Truth regarding gender and sexuality. As we breach these sensitive topics with them, it is of equal importance they see us demonstrate an attitude of love for those who do not embrace God's Truth regarding sexuality and gender, rather than one of harsh judgment. We have the answer the world so desperately needs and it is our job to shine a spotlight on God's grace and mercy.

If your daughter is struggling with gender confusion or same-sex attraction, there are many resources available to guide you. Even if you cannot personally understand or relate to her struggle, that does not mean her struggle is not real. Do not shame her by telling her she shouldn't be feeling those things. It is not a sin to have a same-sex attraction or to experience gender confusion. It is only a sin when it is acted upon. Unfortunately, the church is ill-prepared to minister to those experiencing gender confusion or same-sex attraction. I hope we will see more churches address this topic with grace and humility. The truth is, we are all fighting a battle. Colossians 3:5 calls us to "Put to death therefore what is earthly in you: sexual immorality, impurity, passion, evil desire, and covetousness, which is idolatry" (ESV). We all experience earthly temptations and therefore, we can relate to the struggle to succumb to the culture's lie that fulfilling your desires is the key to happiness. Most of us have learned the hard way that feeding the desires of the flesh can produce misery and bondage.

In 1 Peter 2:11, we are told to "abstain from the passions of the flesh, which wage war against your soul" (ESV). In order to win the battle, we must wage war against that which threatens to defeat us. Whether the battle is a temptation to view pornography, engage in pre-marital sex, have an adulterous affair, act on a same-sex attraction, or declare a different gender, we must have a battle plan in place to protect our souls and experience the abundant life Jesus spoke of in John 10:10. The culture is teaching our children that "if it feels good, do it." We need to be intentional when it comes to dispelling that lie. Part of being intentional is making sure you are discussing this topic with your daughter so she will understand that everyone is facing a battle of some sort when it comes to feeding the desires of the flesh. Even if she is not experiencing the battle, her path will intersect with many who are and she will be better equipped to minister to those who are struggling from a place of compassion and love rather than judgment and shame.

Worth So Much More

If I had to choose one topic to discuss with girls, it would be the topic of worth. The dictionary defines *worth* as "usefulness or importance, as to the world, to a person, or for a purpose." At the core of our being, we all want to feel useful and important to others. We want to know we matter in this great big world we live in. Unfortunately, most of us will look for worth in all the wrong places. I know this because this has been a constant struggle for me over the years.

When I reflect back on the biggest heartaches and struggles of my teen years, I can almost always trace it back to a misdefined sense of worth.

When my esteem plummeted after failing to make the cheer squad in 7th, 9th, and 11th grade: misdefined worth.

When my esteem skyrocketed after making the cheer squad in 8th, 10th, and 12th grade: misdefined worth.

When my friends had a boyfriend in 9th grade and I didn't and I concluded I must be undesirable: misdefined worth.

When one of my friends made a comment about my "big nose" in middle school, I felt ugly and hated my reflection: misdefined worth.

When I engaged in fad starvation diets and ended up with an eating disorder: misdefined worth.

When I drank alcohol with my friends in order to fit in and be cool: misdefined worth.

When I weighed myself several times a day to make sure I hadn't gained a single pound: misdefined worth.

When I obsessed over owning name-brand clothes and accessories in order to impress my peers: misdefined worth.

When I had sex with my high school boyfriend because I
wanted to keep him: misdefined worth.

And the list goes on and on.

Here's the deal about misdefined worth: If you don't reject the
lies you've come to believe and discover where true worth comes
from, you will take that same warped formula for worth into your
adult years. Most of us can attest to that truth. Even those of us who
know better find ourselves lapsing back into the same struggle over
worth. How do our daughters stand a chance if we ourselves are still
engaged in the battle? For starters, we come clean with them and
admit to our struggle. Most of us have subconsciously bought into
the culture's lies regarding worth and rarely question their validity.
It is all we know. Many of us had parents who reinforced the lies,
having ignorantly believed them for themselves. So, what are the
lies regarding worth?

$$Worth = What you look like$$
$$Worth = What you do$$
$$Worth = What others think$$

Not a day goes by that we don't see culture's lie, "Worth = What
you look like" play out. Chances are, your daughter has been on the
receiving end of a compliment or two focused on her appearance.
"She has such a pretty smile." "What a pretty girl!" "She's going to
break a lot of hearts!" "She has such a darling figure!" "She is always
dressed so cute."

There is nothing wrong with commenting on appearance (who
doesn't like to receive a compliment?!), or for that matter, taking
steps to improve our appearance. The problem comes when we
become consumed with it to the point that it begins to define our
worth. If our daughters are conditioned to believe their worth is

related to what they look like on the outside, we set them up for an ongoing battle. What happens when they go through a gangly awkward stage? Or their face breaks out? Or they get a bad haircut? Or they gain weight? What happens if they carry the lie, "Worth = What you look like" into their adult years and their once youthful figure is no longer possible after bearing children? Or they, like us begin the natural aging process and the mirror reminds them daily that beauty does, in fact, fade? If they have been conditioned to believe their worth is dependent on their outer appearance, they will lack worth when their reflection doesn't match their expectations.

Our daughters must be taught that God has a different standard in mind when it comes to worth. Psalm 139:14 reminds us of His standard: "I praise you because I am fearfully and wonderfully made; your works are wonderful, I know that full well." The truth is, if you don't "know that full well," it will be a struggle for you to teach that truth to your daughter. When my daughter was a little girl, I would often stand her up in front of the bathroom mirror and have her say the verse with me. I needed the reminder myself having bought into the lie. In 1 Samuel 16:7, we are reminded that God doesn't value appearance.

> But the LORD said to Samuel, "Do not consider his appearance or his height, for I have rejected him. The LORD does not look at the things people look at. People look at the outward appearance, but the LORD looks at the heart."

God is clear: Worth does not equal what you look like. God cares more about the condition of our hearts. Does your daughter know that? Do you?

Another lie regarding worth is "Worth = What you do." I am the poster child for the long-term damage that can come from believing this lie. It has led to seasons of over-commitment and burnout in my life when I lapse back into believing the lie rather than who I am in Christ. One telltale sign this may be a struggle for you is your calendar. Do you rush to fill empty blocks of time in your day? Is it hard for you to sit still and relax? Have you over-scheduled your children's lives to the point that there is little margin left in your day? Or theirs, for that matter? Do you put an unhealthy emphasis on achievement and success? There is absolutely nothing wrong with looking for ways to cultivate your children's natural gifts and abilities, but the problem comes when there is an unhealthy focus on achievement to the point it begins to define their worth.

What happens when they don't get a ribbon on their science project? Or they fail to make the A team or first string in the sport they have excelled in? Or they fail to make the team at all? Or they get injured and can no longer play? What happens if they fail a test or struggle academically in a subject? What happens if their GPA drops and they fail to make the honor roll or maintain their class ranking? What happens if they don't do well on their college entrance exams and fail to get into the college of their dreams?

God has a different standard when it comes to this lie as well. In Ephesians 2:8–9, we are reminded, "God saved you by his grace when you believed. And you can't take credit for this; it is a gift from God. Salvation is not a reward for the good things we have done, so none of us can boast about it" (NLT). If God doesn't require good works to earn our salvation, He certainly doesn't endorse that our worth be based on our accomplishments. There is nothing wrong with striving for excellence (or for that matter, doing good works), but our worth is not defined by our accomplishments. God never intended that we knock ourselves out like hamsters on a hamster wheel from the cradle to the grave. Life is about so much more than accomplishments and successes. Does your daughter know that? Do you?

Another lie regarding worth is, "Worth = What others think." Look no further than social media to see the power of this lie in play. Every picture and post invite the approval of others. Thumbs up, heart emojis, comments, a friend or follower count. Every day is a popularity contest and it never ends. Your daughter, by default, is growing up in a culture that will let her know what they think whether she likes it or not. Who among us doesn't like approval? It can be a good thing unless our need for it becomes compulsive and our worth becomes dependent on it. The thing is, not everyone will like us and that's *okay*. Sure, sometimes it is beneficial to listen to critics if they're sincere and have our best interests in mind, but oftentimes, we allow the opinions of others to define our worth and value. The apostle Paul spoke to the people-pleasing battle in Galatians 1:10 when he said, "Am I now seeking the approval of man, or of God? Or am I trying to please man? If I were still trying to please man, I would not be a servant of Christ" (ESV). It poses a question for us all: Are we more focused on the approval of men, or of God?

In Psalm 139:17–18, we are reminded, "How precious to me are your thoughts, God! How vast is the sum of them! Were I to count them, they would outnumber the grains of sand." God's thoughts about you outnumber the grains of sand on the shore. Stop and think about that for a minute. We don't have to earn God's approval because He's proved His love for us by sending His Son to die for our sins "while we were still sinners" (Rom. 5:8). When the amazing reality of that sinks in; why in the world would we ever allow the opinions of others to define our worth?! Does your daughter know how God feels about her? Do you know how He feels about you?

If we are to refute the culture's lies regarding worth, we must focus more on the condition of our daughters' hearts than their outer appearance. We must focus more on who they are in Christ rather than their successes, awards and accomplishments. We must focus more on caring less about what others think and more about what God thinks of us. The culture will propagate the worth lies and we can either support the lies or offset the damage by making sure we tell our daughters the truth. For many of us (myself included), it will require a concentrated effort to shift our focus from believing the culture's lies regarding worth to believing God's truth. Old habits die hard, but the freedom that comes from seeing yourself through God's eyes is worth the effort. Do it for your daughter's sake, but also for your sake. You're worth it!

One of my favorite passages of Scripture is Ephesians 3:16–19:

> I pray that out of his glorious riches he may strengthen you with power through his Spirit in your inner being, so that Christ may dwell in your hearts through faith. And I pray that you, being rooted and established in love, may have power, together with all the saints, to grasp how wide and long and high and deep is the love of Christ, and to know this love that surpasses knowledge—that you may be filled to the measure of all the fullness of God. (NIV, 1984)

The Greek word for *filled* in verse 19 is: plērŏō (play-rŏ′-o) and means to "make replete" or to "level up (a hollow)."[4] The passage speaks to the hollow place we all have in our hearts and the necessity to be "rooted and established in love" and further to "grasp how wide and long and high and deep is the love of Christ." Our tendency will be to fill that hollow place with the quick-fix solutions offered by the world whether it be desires, pleasures, impulses, accomplishments, flattery, approval, or the like. While those things may offer a temporary brand of satisfaction, they will not complete us. The buzz will eventually wear off. The unconditional love of God as demonstrated by the love of Christ and His willingness to die for us, is the only thing that will fill the hollow place in our hearts and satisfy us permanently.

If our daughters are to understand their true identity and worth, we must make sure they are rooted and established in God's love. Better yet, we must understand it ourselves and lead by example.

True Biblical Womanhood

Several years ago, I met with a young woman who had been exposed to a dangerous brand of teaching on biblical womanhood. The teacher unapologetically taught that a woman's purpose and destiny as defined by the Bible was to marry, be a helper to her husband, and bear children. In other words, she was taught that she had no identity apart from being a wife and mother. This young woman went on to marry and she and her husband experienced years of infertility. Imagine how painful it was for her to reconcile the shallow and narrow definition of "biblical womanhood" she had been taught. I wish I could tell you stories like this are the exception to the rule, but alas, they are not. Biblical womanhood was never meant to be reduced to a one-size-fits-all destiny that relegated women to be nothing more than wives and mothers.

Biblical womanhood, like biblical manhood is rooted in an identity in Christ rather than the attainment of defined roles. It begins when we are born again and Christ becomes the Lord of our life and thus, our primary affection. A woman who seeks to define her womanhood by God's standards looks to His Word as her final authority. Throughout the Bible we see examples of women who sought the heart of God and changed the course of history. Unfortunately, biblical womanhood is often taught in such a way as to tie the primary identity of a woman to that of being a wife and mother. What does that say for our single women who are single either by choice or circumstances beyond their control or for that matter, women who choose not to or are unable to have children? In its more dangerous form, some teachings related to biblical womanhood (ex: hyper-patriarchal views) suggest that wives are the property of their husbands and are called to be quietly submissive helpmates whose chief aim is to please their husbands. While it is a noble attribute to help and support our husbands in marriage and one we should certainly aspire to (should it be in God's plan to marry), it was never intended to be woman's core identity.

For example, I recently stumbled upon an online video teaching session at a large pastor's conference hosted by an organization that has written volumes on the topic of biblical manhood and biblical womanhood. The teaching session featured a forum where pastors could submit questions in advance to one of four featured experts (also pastors) on the topic of biblical manhood and womanhood. I was shocked to see one pastor on the stage who endorses a narrow and rigid view of biblical womanhood. To give you a little background on his views regarding women, he offered the following marriage advice in a book he wrote: "Wives need to be led with a firm hand. A wife will often test her husband in some area, and be deeply disappointed (and frustrated) if she wins. It is crucial that a husband give to his wife what the Bible says she needs, rather than what she says she needs. So a godly husband is a godly lord. A woman who understands this biblical truth and calls a certain man her husband is also calling him her lord."[5] Nowhere in the Bible does it endorse wives viewing their husbands as "lords" and calling them "lord." Jesus Christ is our only Lord and Savior.

As if that advice wasn't troubling enough, consider this advice he gave in another book: "The first time the dishes are not done, he must sit down with his wife immediately, and gently remind her that this is something which has to be done. . . . He does this, without rancor and without an accusative spirit, until she complies or rebels. If she complies, he must move up one step, now requiring that another of her duties be done. If she continues to rebel after patient effort, he should at some point call the elders of the church and ask them for a pastoral visit."[6] It sounds more like a parent/child relationship where the child in question has been disobedient and unruly, rather than that of a healthy, loving marriage relationship. Not surprisingly, he offered this commentary related to marital sex: "A man penetrates, conquers, colonizes, plants. A woman receives, surrenders, accepts."[7] If that doesn't make the hair stand up on the back of your neck, I don't know what will. Biblical womanhood does not require that women forfeit their voice, surrender their bodies, and give up consent in the process. To suggest that it does would be an endorsement of marital rape.

It saddens me to think of the women who have bought into this brand of biblical womanhood and as a result have forfeited their voices, their gifts and callings, and most of all, their human dignity. Perhaps most disturbing is that upon further research, I was shocked to find that the notable organization hosting the pastor's conference teaches a brand of biblical womanhood that not only rigidly defines the roles a woman can have in the home and church, but also, society at large. In fact, the founder of the ministry (a well-known pastor) that hosted the pastor's event also has another ministry that exists to advise on all matters related to biblical manhood and womanhood. While this pastor has produced many quality materials and resources over the years, he has recently expressed that it is his opinion that women should not be able to teach the Bible to men in seminaries, nor is it advisable for a woman to hold any position in the secular workforce that would involve giving "directives toward men." He cites the specific example of a police officer. Nowhere in the Bible does it say that all women are to submit to all men in all areas of life.

Galatians 3:28 reminds us that with the new covenant, came equality for men and women at the foot of the cross. "There is neither Jew nor Gentile, neither slave nor free, nor is there male nor female, for you are all one in Christ Jesus." You can imagine how radical it must have been for women to be told they were equal in the eyes of God in a day when women were oppressed and considered nothing more than the property of men. You may wonder why this even needs to be said, but it is necessary given that the term "biblical womanhood" has generated much debate over the roles of women both inside and outside of the church. It saddens my heart to think that with all the progress that has been made in recent years to call attention to abuses of power that often place women in vulnerable and at times, abusive situations, there are still teachings circulating in the Christian church and community that treat women as nothing more than submissive doormats who must yield, comply, and keep silent. Jesus Christ was the greatest liberator of all time and set women free from the patriarchal rule that was cultural norm of that day. Women were equal recipients to the gifts poured out on the day of Pentecost and their gifts were never intended to be squelched, denied, or ignored. We need to encourage our daughters to pursue biblical womanhood by defining their identity, worth, and purpose in Christ and Christ alone.

Talk about It

· · · · · · · · · ·

Chapter 1

God reveals his standard for beauty in 1 Samuel 16:7 when he says, "Do not consider his appearance or his height, for I have rejected him. The LORD does not look at the things people look at. People look at the outward appearance, but the LORD looks at the heart."

Would you say you have a tendency to focus more on outward appearance or the heart?

In what ways has your daughter been impacted by the narrow definition of beauty?

In what ways have you been impacted by the culture's narrow definition of beauty?

What are some steps you could take to emphasize inner beauty over outer beauty?

Chapter 2

Has your daughter encountered influences that could encourage her to grow up too fast?

Do you have a tendency to engage in any of the parenting styles listed on pages 30–33?

Which of the key interrupters poses the greatest threat to robbing your daughter of her girlhood?

Chapter 3

Has your daughter encountered a gender-related message or situation that contradicts God's creative order laid out in Genesis 1:27? If so, how did you handle it?

Which of the lies regarding worth is your greatest struggle? What about your daughter?

Worth = What you look like

Worth = What you do

Worth = What others think

In what ways can you be more intentional in modeling for your daughter that worth = who you are in Christ?

Have you been exposed to teachings regarding biblical womanhood that tie a woman's worth to her husband rather than Christ?

Conversation 2

Guard your heart.

Chapter 4

Hooked on Screens

● ● ● ● ● ●

An evil man is held captive by his own sins; they are ropes that catch and hold him. He will die for lack of self-control; he will be lost because of his great foolishness. (Prov. 5:22–23 NLT)

A few years ago, I experienced an intense burnout. Years of juggling back-to-back book deadlines, travel, and ministry obligations finally caught up with me and left me with an unmistakable emptiness in my soul. I knew at the time that if I didn't slow down, catch my breath, and make some necessary changes, the fallout would be immense. As part of my recovery, I had to learn to disconnect from my digital world in order to reconnect to God. As someone who had been an early adapter to technology, I realized I had been sucked into the vortex of screens bidding for my attention from morning to nightfall. Like many of our multi-tasking teens, it wasn't uncommon for me to have a laptop in my lap as I scrambled to make the latest book deadline, my phone by my side to manage my social media accounts, and oftentimes, the TV on in the background. Years of this pattern took a toll on my soul. The problem was only made worse when I would seek escape from the pressures by turning on a 24-hour news show or scrolling through my social media newsfeed. It seemed mindless and innocuous, yet I could not deny that it always seemed to make me feel *worse* rather than *better*. It was just too much. It was then that I realized that at some level, I had allowed technology to master me rather than the other way around. As I began to detox and take steps to limit my media exposure, my overall mental health began to improve.

Technology has completely changed the landscape of the culture in which our children are growing up; smartphones responsible for a large amount of that change. Never before have we had so much information, whether solicited or unsolicited, at our fingertips. And while most of us can remember a time when technology and smartphones weren't a part of everyday life, our children cannot. Many of today's toddlers built their first block tower via an app on Mom's tablet and could swipe through a digital photo library before speaking in sentences. I have a few educational kids' apps on my tablet and I've watched with amazement as my young grandsons know exactly where to find them and have figured out how to play them with little to no direction from me. They, like your children, are early adapters and tech natives.

I myself, can't imagine having to revert back to the days of long-distance phone calls on landlines, busy signals, fold-up maps in the glove box of the car, bulky phone books, record albums, bulky cameras with film cartridges that take twelve, twenty-four, or thirty-six pictures at a time, and encyclopedias (or card catalogs at the library!) to research a topic. As a writer, I wonder how many books would have actually been published if it required me to type them out page by page on a typewriter and correct my mistakes with Liquid Paper! Children today don't know that such a time even existed. Nor do they remember early technology and dial-up Internet that beeped and whined until it connected; if it ever did. This is their world and the challenge will be to raise them to master technology, rather than be mastered by it. But first, we must master it ourselves.

Screen Time and Mental Health

I cannot begin to imagine the impact our tech-saturated culture is having on our children, especially given that their emotional and mental capacity is immature and in a state of constant development. In a way, they are the guinea pigs of a social experiment where constant connectivity has replaced solitude. As true tech natives, they have no other point of reference by which to compare their lives because they have never witnessed a calmer, quieter, unplugged way of life. Most do not even know it is a possibility. Jean Twenge, a professor of psychology at San Diego State University, has devoted much of her study to the generations, past and current and believes it is "not an exaggeration to describe iGen as being on the brink of the worst mental-health crisis in decades."[1] One of the sources she cites that led her to this conclusion is *The Monitoring the Future* survey, which is funded by the National Institute on Drug Abuse. The survey has asked twelfth-graders more than 1,000 questions every year since 1975 and queried eighth- and tenth-graders since 1991. The survey gauges leisure time and how it is spent and more importantly, the impact it has on their happiness. In recent years, it has taken a much closer look on screen activities such as using social media, texting, and browsing the web, and Twenge claims,

"The results could not be clearer: Teens who spend more time than average on screen activities are more likely to be unhappy, and those who spend more time than average on non-screen activities are more likely to be happy. There's not a single exception. All screen activities are linked to less happiness, and all non-screen activities are linked to more happiness."[2]

Not surprisingly, the risk of unhappiness due to social media use is the highest for the youngest teens. Eighth-graders who spent ten or more hours a week on social networking sites were 56 percent more likely to be unhappy, compared to 47 percent for tenth-graders and 20 percent for twelfth-graders.[3] Eighth-graders who are heavy users of social media increase their risk of depression by 27 percent, while those who play sports, go to religious services, or even do homework more than the average teen cut their risk significantly.[4] Even more disturbing is the finding that "teens who spend three hours a day or more on electronic devices are thirty-five percent more likely to have a risk factor for suicide, such as making a suicide plan."[5]

In addition to reporting record levels of unhappiness among teens, the survey also found that teens are now lonelier than at any other times since the survey began in 1991.[6] Stop and think about that for a moment. The generation with the ability to connect with hundreds of people around the clock through social media is the loneliest and most disconnected generation on record. If that isn't a wake-up call, I don't know what is. And it's only increasing. The survey found that "a stunning thirty-one percent more eighth and tenth graders felt lonely in 2015 than in 2011, along with twenty-two percent more twelfth graders."[7] Twenge notes, "Such large changes over a short period of time are unusual, suggesting a specific cause with a big impact. Given the timing, smartphones are the most likely culprits, increasing loneliness both directly and indirectly replacing in-person social interaction."[8]

The American Freshman Survey which surveys entering college students found similar results. Twenge notes, "Every indicator of mental health issues on the survey reached all-time highs in 2016—rating emotional health below average (increasing 18 percent since 2009), feeling overwhelmed (increasing 51 percent), expecting to seek counseling (increasing 64 percent), and—perhaps most troubling—feeling depressed (increasing 95 percent, or nearly doubling), with noticeable jumps just between 2015 and 2016."[9] She goes on to say, "In 2016, for the first time, the majority of entering college students described their mental health as below average. The sudden, sharp rise in depressive symptoms occurred at almost exactly the same time that smartphones became ubiquitous and in-person interaction plummeted."[10] If you need any more proof, consider also that The National Survey on Drug Use and Health (NSDUH), which is conducted by the US Department of Health and Human Services, has screened more than 17,000 teens (ages twelve to seventeen) across the country every year for clinical-level depression since 2004. The screening results show an escalating rise in depression in a very short period of time, reporting that 56 percent more teens experienced a major depressive episode in 2015 than in 2010.[11]

It is not just our teens who are at risk. Other studies have found that the more TV a child watches between the ages of one and three, the greater the likelihood that they will develop an attention problem by age seven, and six- to twelve-year-olds who spent more than two hours a day playing video games or watching TV had trouble paying attention in school and were more likely to have attention problems.[12]

Dr. Victoria Dunckley—a child psychiatrist specializing in electronic screen syndrome after having worked with countless children with psychiatric, developmental, and behavioral disorders—began to take a closer look at possible underlying causes in an effort to explain the uptick in mental health disorders among children. "As she looked at the data, she saw that visits for kids diagnosed with pediatric bipolar disorder had increased 40-fold from 1994 to 2003; that between 1980 and 2007 the diagnosis of ADHD had increased by nearly 80 percent, while prescriptions for psychotropic medications given to kids had sharply increased over the past two decades."[13] As Dr. Dunckley began to parse through the data, she discovered a common denominator in play: screens.

The Brain Science Behind the Compulsion

Dr. Nicholas Kardaras, an addictions expert and author of the book, *Glow Kids: How Screen Addiction Is Hijacking Our Kids*, notes that "recent brain-imaging studies conclusively show that excessive screen exposure can neurologically damage a young person's developing brain in the same way that cocaine addiction can."[14] Kardaras does an amazing job of explaining the brain science behind the compulsive nature many kids have when it comes to their screens, whether it be computers, phones, TV's, video games, or the like. Much like an electronic drug, our kids receive a dopamine blast in the reward center of their brains that keep them coming back for more and more of the same. It can be triggered by achieving the next level in a computer or video game, receiving likes or positive comments on pictures posted on social media, or viewing pornography and other technology stimulants. Some kids have a temperament or genetic influence that puts them at greater risk for addiction. Kardaras notes, "We know that having addiction in one's family can predispose a person toward that condition and that the children of addicts are eight times more likely to develop an addiction problem."[15]

Perhaps even more disturbing is that the social media and video game industries are well aware of the brain science that can lead many individuals (especially, young vulnerable children) to get "hooked" on their products and services. "Gaming companies will hire the best neurobiologists and neuroscientists to hook up electrodes to the test-gamer. If they don't elicit the blood pressure that they shoot for—typically 180 over 120 or 140 within a few minutes of playing, and if they don't show sweating and an increase in their galvanic skin responses, they go back and tweak the game to get that maximum addicting and arousing response that they're looking for."[16] Add to this that a former Facebook president recently admitted the site was built to exploit "a vulnerability in human psychology." Sean Parker admitted that when he and the team launched Facebook in the early 2000s, they were trying to figure out, "How do we consume as much of your time and conscious attention as possible?" He goes on to add, "It literally changes your relationship with society, with each other." Parker adds, "God only knows what it's doing to our children's brains."[17] Our kids may not be on Facebook much anymore (if at all), but rest assured that the latest and greatest social media platform has also figured out how to exploit the same vulnerability in human psychology.

By now, you're probably wanting to gather up all the screens in your house and use them for target practice in the backyard. It's important to remember that technology is not a bad thing. In fact, we enjoy its benefits on a daily basis and it has, on many occasions, enriched our lives. The problem lies in how we choose to utilize it. I personally have loved reconnecting with old friends (thanks to social media!) and have enjoyed many of the other benefits it has provided such as staying in touch with friends and family members, and hearing from many of the women who have read my books. I have figured out how it can best serve me rather than the other way around. As depressing as many of these findings are, I am hopeful that it will expose our desperate need for a different kind of connection. God wired our hearts for connection with Him, first and foremost. Secondly, it is His desire that we connect with others in a deep and meaningful way. Perhaps this is the wake-up call for parents to talk with their children about their deep-seated need for connection with God, so they are not as likely to fall for a false substitute.

The Spiritual Impact of a Media-Consumed Life

In Luke chapter 10, we see a picture of the spiritual tug-of-war our souls are engaged in on a daily basis with the example of two sisters, Mary and Martha. Jesus was a guest in their home and while Mary "sat at the Lord's feet and listened to is teaching," Martha, we are told, "was distracted with much serving" (vv. 39–40 ESV). While the clear link to excessive media-consumption and mental health will compel many parents to draw limits on their children's access, Christian parents should be far more concerned with the impact it will have on the spiritual health of their children. You can't catch God on the run and expect to have a thriving, deep relationship with Him. Getting to know Christ will require silence, solitude, and stillness.

In his book, *12 Ways Your Phone Is Changing You*, author Tony Reinke proposes that we engage in digital distractions to "keep thoughts of eternity away."[18] He goes on to cite the wisdom of seventeenth-century Christian mathematician Blaise Pascal who theorized we are easily lured by distractions in an effort to avoid having to be alone with ourselves. "I have discovered that all the unhappiness of men arises from one single fact, that they cannot stay quietly in their own chamber. Hence it comes that men so much love noise and stir; hence it comes that the prison is so horrible a punishment; hence it comes that the pleasure of solitude is a thing incomprehensible."[19] How ironic that the weariness of our souls can be cured by seeking Christ and sitting at His feet and yet, much like the fickle Israelites, we choose instead to chase after our own modern-day false gods. Truth be told, this is not an issue that impacts our children. It impacts us all, regardless of age and spiritual maturity. Maybe your false gods go by different names than your children's, but the damage is the same. If they succeed in claiming your ongoing attention and more dangerously, your ongoing affection, there will be little margin left in your life to cultivate a relationship with God.

God encourages us to lay our hearts bare before Him, and yet that is the very thing many of us are trying to avoid. "Put me on trial, LORD, and cross-examine me. Test my motives and my heart" (Ps. 26:2 NLT). We are afraid to meet Him in the silence and quiet of our lives for fear of what He may show us. How ironic that the distractions we chase are false substitutes and will ultimately rob us of the One thing our hearts truly crave: intimacy with God. To know Him and be known by Him. Nothing else will do. We need to help our children recognize the emptiness that ensues in this meaningless chase and be faithful to point them to the cure. But first, we must admit our own susceptibility to the chase.

What's a Parent to Do?

While recently on a dinner date with my husband, I couldn't help but notice the number of people sitting at nearby tables looking at their phones rather than each other. In fact, at one table an entire family of four were each engaged on their own separate devices and oblivious of one another's company. The kids couldn't have been more than ten to twelve years old and while the older daughter was scrolling away on a phone, her younger brother had earbuds in and was playing a game on a tablet. Across from them, Mom and Dad were engaged on their own phones, tuned out to their surroundings, each other, and more importantly, their children. I couldn't help but feel a heaviness in my heart. With Mom and Dad leading by example, the kids don't stand a chance when it comes to experiencing the joy of true face-to-face friendship and intimacy. What a lonely existence and this was their "family time"!

Contrast this image to another one I witnessed later that same week when my husband and I went to lunch with a pastor and his family after I had spoken at their church on a Sunday morning. Their children were about the same age as the other children I had witnessed earlier that week and there were no devices present. They listened to the adult conversation, politely engaged from time to time, and when they grew weary of the lingering conversation after the food had been served and consumed, they asked their parents politely if they could read their books! It had never occurred to them to beg for their parents' phone because they had clearly been taught that mealtime was a tech-free zone.

I get it. I know it's tempting to hand your kids a device to gain a little peace and quiet or have a little uninterrupted conversation with your spouse or other adults, but it should be the exception rather than the rule. Establishing tech-free zones are a good first start to limiting media consumption. In addition, resist the pull to give your children devices and privileges too soon. I know this will be hard when many of their friends are allowed earlier media access or handed devices. Hold strong. Likewise, don't ban all technology out of fear and swing too far in the other direction. Ephesians 6:4 reminds us, "Fathers, do not provoke your children to anger, but bring them up in the discipline and instruction of the Lord" (ESV). *Matthew Henry's Commentary* expounds on the verse in saying, "Be not impatient; use no unreasonable severities. Deal prudently and wisely with children; convince their judgments and work upon their reason. Bring them up well; under proper and compassionate correction; and in the knowledge of the duty God requires." If you issue an all-out ban on all technology and allow your children no privileges, I can assure you it will provoke them to anger. Unreasonable severities doled out by parents oftentimes backfire. (Think here, the law of forbidden fruit.) Like it or not, technology is here to stay. The best time for your child to learn to manage it is when they are under your roof and you can guide them to use it responsibly. Expect that there will be many bumps along the way. You may extend privileges only to learn it was too soon and then have to withdraw them. You are the parent and you have that right.

I especially love the advice in the commentary above to "convince their judgments and work upon their reason." Be honest with your children from the time they are young and help them understand the link to too much media consumption and mental health, so they know the "why" behind your "wait." When you frame the conversation of media privileges as one of care and concern for their mental health and welfare, they are better able to understand why you may have rules in place that many of their friends' parents do not. Another way to "work upon their reason" is to talk to them about over-consumption of media and the link to unhappiness. For iGen children, happiness ranked as a top goal for a majority. Help them to recognize that heavy media consumption is causing an epidemic of unhappiness among their generation.

Once you feel they are old enough to have a taste of certain forms of media, approach with a training wheels approach. Just as you would never put a toddler on a ten-speed bike and let them loose in the bad part of town, likewise, you shouldn't expose your child, tween, or teen to a situation they are not mature enough to manage. Just as you would help your little one on a bike with training wheels and run alongside them as they get a feel for learning to ride a bike, you should also come alongside your child when they begin engaging with technology and especially, social media. Postpone handing them devices with Internet access (tablets, smartphones, gaming systems, laptops) for as long as possible, especially if you are not there to supervise them. When my children began to engage in social media, I required all of their passwords to their social media accounts and spot-checked their devices on occasion, as well as installing monitoring software on many of their devices. I'm sure they still managed to get around some of my boundaries of protection, but just knowing I was determined to be an engaged parent had to be somewhat of a deterrent. Or so I tell myself!

The truth is, if a child wants to get away with something, they will find a way to do it. We cannot monitor their behavior every minute of every day, but we can educate them about the dangers of too much media consumption and the link to mental health issues that have become all too common among children and teens. We can have open and honest conversations about our struggle with media consumption and the pull it has on our lives. Most importantly, we can expose our children to other fulfilling activities that will give them taste for true intimacy and quality family time. Technology can be a good thing. It is not the enemy, but it can quickly become the enemy if we allow it to have too much power in our lives or the lives of our children. Some children are more prone than others to screen addictions and for those, it can be a challenge to wean them off screens or reduce their time spent on screens. If you fear your child might be addicted to screens, I've included a list of symptoms in the appendix.

Most children will not fall into the addiction category, but many if not most, will struggle with finding a healthy balance when it comes to media consumption. As parents, we must help them learn to self-monitor and recognize the warning signs of technology-induced anxiety, loneliness, and depression and take necessary steps to pull back or unplug when it gets to be too much. Most importantly, we must constantly remind them that the FOMO factor ("fear of missing out") that compels them to connect digitally whether it be mindless surfing of the web, social media, texting, online gaming, binge-watching Netflix, or any other media escape is ironically misplaced. Excess media consumption is causing them to miss out on the things that matter most!

If after reading this chapter you feel that a digital detox is in order for your child (or yourself), consider unplugging for a couple of weeks in order to prove you are not mastered by technology. You will not die. Your child will not die. In fact, it may be the very thing that enables them to begin living again. Experts recommend 4–6 weeks if the problem is severe in order that the nervous system can effectively reset itself. Consider joining your child if possible. During the detox period, help your child find other activities or interests, preferably outdoors. Do what you can to expose your child to others during this time, whether it be friends or family members.

One question I've learned to ask myself on a regular basis when engaging with technology is: "Is this good for my soul?" When the answer is "no," it's up to me to do something about it. No one else is going to come along and fix the problem for me. The same is true for our children. We can draw boundaries and take steps to monitor their media consumption, but at the end of the day, they have to come to a place where they care more about the condition of their souls than we do. They will have to decide whether or not they will master the technology that influences their lives, or be mastered by it. For the sake of their mental health. For the sake of their spiritual health. For the sake of their souls.

Chapter 5

The Friendship Factor

● ● ● ● ● ●

The righteous choose their friends carefully, but the way
of the wicked leads them astray. (Prov. 12:26)

One of the single greatest influences in our daughters' growing up years will be their peer group. When they are young, their early friendships develop organically, whether they are mom-initiated or result from being in the same homeroom. As our daughters mature and become more capable of exercising independent thought, we begin to see them take a more active approach to choosing their friends. They will naturally seek out those they most identify with, or for some girls, those they *desire to* identify with. They may even experiment with several different peer groups until they find a good match. At this point, they may choose to part ways with the friends they had in the earlier years or, in some cases, the friends we handpicked for them. This can be especially difficult if some of their old friends just so happen to be "family friends."

The type of friends your daughter chooses or gravitates toward can speak volumes about her developing identity. It's hard to say whether "identity determines peer group" or "peer group determines identity," but the point is really moot. Either way your daughter has willingly chosen to identify with a peer group; and, depending on the nature of that peer group, it can have a positive or negative outcome on her behavior and the choices she makes. For this reason, it is important to give our daughters the tools to properly discern between healthy friendships and unhealthy friendships in an effort to guard and protect their hearts.

If you have a daughter in middle school or older, you've probably witnessed the dramatic shift that takes place when it comes to the importance of friendships. During these years our daughters begin to prioritize peer approval over parent approval. And if the shift caught you off guard as it did me, be encouraged that studies confirm that it's not personal. Ginny Olson notes in her book *Teenage Girls: Exploring Issues Adolescent Girls Face and Strategies to Help Them*, that it's important for mothers to realize that "although their daughters may seem to be distancing themselves, they aren't seeking total autonomy." She goes on to share the results of research by Dr. Terri Apter of the University of Cambridge, who has studied mothers and daughters for more than twenty years. In her research she found that daughters aren't seeking a "divorce" from their mothers; rather, they're seeking to redefine the relationship in the midst of their changing world. Apter states, "The 'task' of adolescence is not to sever the closeness, but to alter it."[1]

This transition can often catch mothers off guard. I remember back years ago when I was doing mother/daughter events and witnessed this sudden shift in girls preferring the company of their friends over their mothers. At events where tween and teen girls were present, the younger girls would sit with their mothers and openly show them affection. The older girls on the other hand, typically sat in a group with their friends at a safe distance away from their mothers and any mother that dared to approach was guaranteed a sharp glare in return. It was almost as if our adoring daughters went to bed one night thinking we had hung the moon and woke up the next day thinking we were from the moon. I remember the transition well and am happy to report that for most mothers and daughters, it is a temporary stage or pause, if you will, in the friendship.

When my daughter moved 800 miles away from home to attend college out of state, all of a sudden, I became cool again. She needed me once again and hardly a day goes by that we don't talk to each other. In fact, she only lives three miles from my house! She is raising her own daughter now, and I tease her on occasion about those days when she didn't much like me and remind her that her turn is coming! If I could go back and have a little talk with my younger mom self, I'd tell that mom that her daughter will come back and it will be a sweet relationship once again. Unfortunately, as part of the maturity process, it is necessary that our daughters gradually pull away in an effort to assert their independence. Mothers who understand this will not take it personally when that day comes.

Weekday versus Weekend Friends

When our daughters are young, they need our help when it comes to developing healthy friendships. One distinction we made in our home was the difference between "weekday friends" and "weekend friends." A "weekday friend" might be someone our child met at school or through an extracurricular activity. If our child expressed an interest in a new friend and we didn't know much about the child or the climate of their home-life, we encouraged play dates at our home until we could get to know the child and their parents. This helped protect our child against those awkward moments that can come when there is a different value system in place at a friend's house. Many children today are allowed to access the Internet without supervision or watch shows that you may not allow your child to watch. By limiting play dates to our home in the early years in these uncertain situations, it affords you the opportunity to monitor the friendship all the while preparing your child to speak up when there is a conflict of values.

In comparison, a "weekend friend" was a friend whose family shared similar beliefs and values as our family. We knew the parents and had a peace that should our child spend time at the friend's home, the parents would, for the most part, be on the same page regarding many of the outside influences that often rush our children to grow up.

Obviously, the "weekend friend" list was a much shorter list than the "weekday friend" list. Having taught our children that distinction, we had a baseline for helping them navigate new friendships while under a protective and watchful eye. As they got older, we relaxed the rules once we felt they were able to speak up when a friend might suggest something they were forbidden to do in our home. I can recall my daughter calling me on many occasions from friends' houses asking for permission to watch movies that were rated for a more mature audience. Sometimes I relented, depending on the material in question and other times, I did not. I encouraged my children to resolve the matter rather than micro-manage the situation and contact the parents. I wouldn't always be there to manage the situation, so the goal was to equip them to speak up. As hard as it might be for our children to take that initiative, it better prepares them to speak up in the teen years when presented with tempting situations.

When our children entered the high school years, we opened our home and were happy to be a designated teen hangout. I have great memories of those days and loved getting to know my children's friends. This was especially helpful when they began driving and were less content to hang out at someone's house. By that point, we had a fairly good gauge on our children's peer groups. As social media has become more of the connecting force in our children's lives, it has become more difficult to distinguish their true friends from their virtual friends. It was much easier to monitor our children's friend groups when they were hanging out in our homes rather than online via their smartphones and tablets. That doesn't mean we give up and accept defeat. Monitor your daughter's accounts and spot-check her devices from time to time to get an idea of who her online peer group is. Remind her often that real friendships are built face-to-face and offline. Studies show that teens are spending more time connecting online than in person, so you may have to nudge your daughter to initiate getting together with a friend or two. Setting limits on her media consumption will encourage her to hang out with friends in person rather than online.

Do whatever it takes to make it possible for your daughters to spend time with girls who share the same values and would make good "weekend friends." My daughter moved from a small private school to a large public school when she began high school and had a difficult transition when it came to finding friends who shared the same values. She spent many weekends at home during those first couple of years; and while it certainly spared her from many temptations, it was difficult for her all the same. During those years

I did whatever I could to help her maintain contact with some of her friends from her old private school (on one side of town) as well as our youth group (the other side of town) who had proven to be good, solid friends over the years. Eventually, she was able to drive and connect with them on her own. They were scattered about in their college years but have since reunited as young wives and mothers and get together regularly. The effort was well worth it.

Identifying High-Risk Friends

The National Longitudinal Study of Adolescent Health surveyed more than ninety thousand adolescents on many health-related issues and evaluated peer influence (specifically related to teen pregnancy). The study found that, on average, a girl's risk of pregnancy decreased one percentage point for every one percent increase in low-risk friends versus high-risk friends she has in her peer group. The study also noted that a couple of high-risk female friends in a girl's crowd are not that dangerous and do not necessarily hasten first intercourse or increase the risk of pregnancy.[2] The key, rather, seems to rest on having a majority of low-risk friends.

On the other hand, having high-risk male friends and older friends of both sexes increases girls' risk of negative behaviors. And while having low-risk male friends is protective, high-risk male friends may place girls at heightened risk for pregnancy.[3] Again, this study focused specifically on peer group and the influence of pregnancy; however, I think their conclusions can be applied across the board to other dangerous behaviors that can have life-altering consequences. Benjamin Franklin once said, "He who lies down with the dogs, shall rise up with fleas." If you've ever had to treat a flea-infested dog, I think you'll agree that it's far better to take preventive measures on the front end than to tackle the problem after the fact.

My husband and I were committed to monitoring our children's peer groups. When we identified high-risk friends, we were equally as committed to discouraging the friendship, or at the very least, limiting contact or putting it on hold. Our youngest son was our greatest challenge and required the closest monitoring. His personality was impulsive and he was more of a people-pleaser than his siblings were, which is the perfect storm for high-risk behaviors. We even transferred him to a smaller private school halfway through high school to put him in a smaller environment where we could better monitor his peer group. In other words, we made it as difficult as possible for him to run with the wrong crowd. We openly talked to him about his tendency to be a "follower" rather than a "leader," and tried to guide him toward friendships that would not put him in compromising situations. It was exhausting at the time, and though we could not perfectly protect him (most often, from himself!), we have no regrets. He still had to learn some tough lessons the hard way, but it could have been so much worse.

As a parent, you have every right to have a vote when it comes to your daughter's choice in friends. If your daughter runs with a crowd that is eager to grow up, she will behave in a like manner. Encourage your daughter to spend time with girls who are comfortable acting their age. It may be necessary in some cases to ban your daughter completely from high-risk associations for a season (or sometimes permanently) when boundary lines are crossed or trust is breached. My husband and I have always prayed that if (when) our children strayed from the path of God, they would be caught in their sin as early as possible. Simply put, we asked God to sound the sin alarm to "Repent! Turn back!" Should our children respond by hitting the snooze button, we wanted them caught so we could intervene in an effort to: (1) address the problem at its root cause, and (2) protect them from straying any further down the path before they develop a negative habit or pattern. In a nutshell we wanted them caught before they could hit the snooze button.

One of my sons had a wake-up call in the summer prior to his junior year of high school. He lied about their whereabouts in order to attend a party where alcohol was present (and consumed). Just as we had prayed, he was caught and as a result, immediately placed on lockdown. In addition to seizing his cell phone, laptop, and car keys (with the exception of driving to school and work), we also banned him from associating with anyone else who had been involved in the situation until we could get a better grasp on the situation (this included several of his church friends). We reasoned that these "friends" were not a good influence on our child; and our child was in turn not a good influence on them.

Because a breach of trust had occurred, the burden of responsibility was placed on our son to earn the trust back before privileges were reinstated. I know this sounds harsh, but given the power of peer influence, we have a responsibility to protect our children. Sometimes this means drawing boundaries that would aid in protecting them from *themselves*. Sometimes a "friend intervention" is a much-needed wake-up call to rouse our child from a spiritual slumber.

The Truth about Church Kids

My daughter, unlike her younger brother, was more of a compliant, rule-follower, and risk-averse in her personality. She naturally sought out similar types of friends who had no interest in being on the fast track. Our oldest son was more of an introvert and sought out a few close friends, which made monitoring his peer group much easier. I share that to say that your child's personality and temperament will be a huge factor in determining whether or not they are at a higher risk of falling into the wrong crowd. That said, I want to caution against making the assumption that "church kids" are not as likely to engage in high-risk behaviors. Sometimes, they are the ones leading the charge!

The truth is, many of the church kids are equally as susceptible to temptations as non-church kids. Studies show there is little difference in the rate of churched and non-churched teens engaging in sex, binge drinking, and other high-risk behaviors, so don't falsely assume that just because your child's friend(s) are church kids, they share the same Christian values and are less likely to engage in risky behaviors. A recent Barna study surveyed 1,490 US teens ages thirteen to eighteen and asked if they believed moral issues including lying, recreational use of marijuana, sex outside of marriage, abortion, and homosexuality were wrong. Sadly, they found that there was little difference in the answers from "Churched Christian" teens and "Unchurched Christian" teens.[4] However, there was a distinct difference in the answers from "Engaged Christian" teens. Unfortunately, only 9 percent of teens fell into the category of "Engaged Christian" teen. (We'll talk more about what constitutes the "Engaged Christian" category in chapter 14 and, more importantly, the role parents play.) Think about that. If you walk into your youth group on any given Sunday morning, only about one in eleven students hold views that are consistent with a biblical worldview. This is certainly a wake-up call for Christian parents who have developed a false sense of security by assuming their child's church friends are a better influence than other kids they associate with. Clearly, that's not always the case.

My daughter had a friend in high school who was not a "church kid," but she had caring engaged parents who shared many of the same values we did. Like my daughter, she had no interest in the rush to grow up. They went on to make the cheer squad together and become the best of friends. They separated after graduation to attend different colleges, but reunited after college to be each other's maids-of-honor when they married. Today, they are young mothers and get together with their daughters for play dates. I could not have picked a better friend for my daughter.

The Never-Ending Party

When I was growing up, there was a public service announcement that ran every night before the evening news began. It said, "It's ten-o-clock. Do you know where your children are?" I suppose it speaks to the free-range parenting philosophy that was more common among Boomer parents. Today's generation of kids is the safest generation to date and yet, ironically most of their parents have no idea where their kids are even if they are physically down the hall in their bedroom. If they have a smartphone, tablet, or laptop, they can be hanging out with their friends and exposed to peer pressures we can't even begin to imagine. Sexting, porn, you name it—it's all right there under your roof. Your child doesn't have to sneak out to go to the party; the party has come to her. Even if your daughter is making good choices, if she is connected to the party, she has likely witnessed many of these risky behaviors among her friends or other virtual friends who may not even be in her immediate peer group. This is especially true if your daughter is allowed access on any of the social media platforms where parents have been shut out and cannot see pictures and video clips that disappear in a matter of seconds. You may be able to trust your daughter, but can you really trust all the other kids she's connected to on these apps? More importantly, at what point does she become desensitized to what she is seeing?

George Washington once said, "Associate yourself with men of good quality if you esteem your own reputation. It is better to be alone than in bad company." If my kids were growing up with access to apps like this, I would likely have banned them due to the fact that there is no way to monitor what others are posting. Add to that the clear link of mental health issues related to excessive and compulsive screen time. At the very least, I encourage you to postpone the use of social media apps for as long as possible and require login and passwords and spot-check her account on a regular basis to make sure you're comfortable with the decision. Be aware that many teens are setting up fake social media accounts ("finstas") to escape prying parents who are monitoring their real one. Have frequent and candid conversations with your daughter about your expectations and the consequences that will occur should she not abide by your rules. At the end of the day, you're the parent and you have every right to shut down the party if it gets out of hand.

Finding a Healthy Balance

One of the most difficult parenting challenges is when other parents allow their children to have or do things you're not comfortable allowing your children to have or do. It can make for a stressful situation in your home, especially if your child is the only one in her peer group who is not allowed the privilege. The goal is to find a balance that protects your child without breaking their spirit in the process. Parents who go overboard in drawing too many boundaries, and making it a habit to say "no" to most everything, run the risk that their children will sneak around to participate in many of the things their friends are doing. The more you deny something, the more determined your child is to possess it. Trust me when I say I've witnessed this phenomenon in many Christian homes that had the best of intentions. This is especially true once the child leaves the nest and has their first taste of unmonitored freedom.

In our home, we tried (often through trial and error) to find a healthy balance that sought to land in the middle on many issues where our children wanted to engage in an activity that their friends were allowed to engage in. Whether it was a decision related to an appropriate age to have a cell phone, engage in social media, date, attend after-prom parties, or one of the many decisions that oftentimes caught us off guard, we tried to choose our battles for the sake of winning the bigger war. Oftentimes, instead of issuing a firm "no," we looked for ways to come alongside our children and supervise the activity in question, all the while reserving the right to reverse our decision should we decide it was too much, too soon. This was also our approach when it came to our children's friends and peer group. It took time and effort to be involved and engaged in getting to know their friends as well as their friends' parents. We did not expect perfection, nor did we expect that we would always see eye-to-eye with other parents.

When we had to issue a "no" on a particular friend or an activity in question, we tried to explain the "why" behind our "no." Most often it boiled down to a decision to protect our child from a friend or activity where we determined there was an increased likelihood that our child would be exposed to high-risk behaviors. Our children had firm curfews, weren't allowed to do coed sleepovers (yes, this is a thing), and we unapologetically monitored their devices and social media accounts until we felt each one had proven that they could be trusted with the privilege. At times, I wanted to give up because it was exhausting and felt, at times, out of my control. All that to say, I have zero regrets and would do it all over again. It would have been far easier at the time to have given my children no boundaries and let the chips fall where they may. Plenty of parents operated by that philosophy and ended up having to sweep up an even bigger mess on down the road, or for lack of a better term, had to re-parent their kids after the fact.

The truth is, we can't protect our daughters twenty-four hours a day from making foolish choices, but we *can* set up boundaries and rules to make it more difficult for them to make foolish choices. And we can certainly limit their exposure to situations where other parents are contributing to the pursuit of foolishness by failing to supervise the children in their care.

The One Relationship That Matters Most

The verdict is in. The most connected generation on the planet is hopelessly *lonely*. With all their friends, followers, and 24/7 access to a never-ending party, they are left empty and wanting for more. Could it be that the same God who wired our hearts first and foremost to connect with Him, also wired our same hearts to connect more deeply with fewer people? How I wish we could give this generation of tech natives a glimpse into the future ten to twenty years from now and show them how insignificant their digital connections will be. Even better if we could show them a tally of the total amount of accumulated time they spent engaging or interacting with these insignificant friends on social media in their younger years. I imagine many would weep at the reality of the wasted time that could have been better spent on relationships that mattered—first with their Creator, and then with their family members and real friends.

I know it's not likely we can get them to recognize the futility of it all, but we can be faithful in talking openly about the emptiness that comes from attempting to fill that void in their hearts with false substitutes. Only when they recognize that emptiness and decide to take steps on their own to self-monitor will they find true rest for their souls. That's where the gospel comes in. Jesus is the only thing that will satisfy their hearts and no amount of virtual friends and shallow round-the-clock connections will ever come close. In the meantime, we can draw boundaries, set limits, monitor their peer group, and nudge them toward the only Friend who will stand the test of time.

Chapter 6

Boy, Oh Boy

● ● ● ● ● ●

*Daughters of Jerusalem, I charge you: Do not arouse or
awaken love until it so desires. (Song of Solomon 8:4)*

If there had been a Boy Crazy Club in grade school, I would have
been the president. I can't recall the exact moment boys appeared
on my radar, but I'm pretty certain I can trace it back to the "I like
you" note that I passed Bill Anderson in my fourth-grade homeroom
class. When he replied back in his fourth-grade boy-scribble admit-
ting that he liked me too, I passed it around to all my best girlfriends
who, in turn, responded by finding their own boy to pass a note to.
It was as if our cooties inoculations had simultaneously worn off
and a new truce had been called. These same annoying creatures
that had at one time made our skin crawl now mysteriously made
our hearts beat faster and our cheeks flush when they so much as
glanced in our general direction or breathed our same air.

Maybe boys didn't make it on your radar as early as fourth grade, but I'm betting you still have memories of when it did. And as hard as it is to imagine, your daughter will chalk up plenty of her own memories when it comes to cooties, crushes, and all things boys. Yet in spite of the fact that this is a normal occurrence in the growing-up process, most mothers will be completely and totally caught off guard when it occurs, unsure of how to respond or react. Seriously, where is the guidebook to delineate all the details?

As someone who has been in ministry to both girls and mothers through the years, I am happy to share some observations I have made along the way regarding this sometimes-controversial subject. In addition, now that my own daughter has journeyed through middle school, high-school, college, and taken a walk down the aisle to say "I do," I am a firm believer in the dating model we had in our home. There are many different attitudes regarding the topic of boy-girl relationships, especially when it comes to what is appropriate and acceptable for Christian kids. Some of you reading this chapter will think my approach is too conservative. Others of you may think my approach is too liberal. The important thing is that you take the matter before the Lord and come up with a plan of your own that best suits your daughter's temperament. Proverbs 15:22 says, "Plans fail for lack of counsel, but with many advisers they succeed." Just view me as one of many advisers. You know your daughter best, and what has worked for my daughter may not work for your daughter. But this much I do know: Have a plan and, preferably, get it in place before boys show up on her radar.

Grammar School: Innocent Curiosity

Oh, how I wish an older, wiser mother had taken me aside when I was laboring over the episodes of young love in my home and told me to take a chill pill. When I look back and think of all the hand-wringing I experienced over trying to decide if my son should be allowed to buy the girl he liked in fifth grade a stuffed animal for Valentine's Day or whether my daughter should be allowed to send the boy she likes a note from summer camp, I want to slap myself silly. Trust me when I say that you can overanalyze some topics, and this is one of them. When all was said and done, all three of my children experienced the thrill of "young love" at some basic level and had a few stuffed animals and love notes to show for it in the end. And shock of shocks, the world continued to rotate on its axis.

It is perfectly normal for girls at this age to have crushes and even talk about "boyfriends." Kids often model what they see around them and just as your daughter may have taken an interest in dressing-up or pretending to be a mom with her dolls, she is iden-tifying with a role. Try not to tease your daughter about liking boys or having a boyfriend, but rather, put the focus on "friendships" with boys in the grammar school years.

Middle School: Boys on the Radar

I was pretty low-key when it came to the experimental phase of "going out." My mantra during those years was, "You can call it going out, but you're not going anywhere!" Of course, they were required to hang out in groups, and no couple time was allowed. Ever. With my two older children, their experimental going-out phase was fairly uneventful and, quite honestly, resulted in their clamming up and talking less with the other person once the relationship officially transitioned to the "going out" status.

My younger son had a slightly different journey with his going-out experiences since texting had become more prevalent by the time he entered middle school. Because kids felt more comfortable typing and texting things they wouldn't normally say to someone's face, it removed the natural barrier of awkwardness that was common when learning to communicate with the opposite sex. I encourage you to have some boundaries in place for communication with the opposite sex, regardless of whether you allow your child to "go out." I also recommend that you consider limiting or banning text messaging and possibly even taking the phone up at night. I did this for a time when I discovered that girls were texting my youngest son at all hours of the night in his eighth-grade year. Even if your daughter is responsible enough to be trusted with the responsibility, there is no way to control what others may send her.

Also, I highly recommend that you not allow your daughter to participate in the social networking sites unless you have the time to carefully monitor her activity. The minimum age on some sites is fourteen, but many middle schoolers are lying about their ages or setting up secret accounts in order to participate in this forum. If you are considering allowing your daughter to participate in texting or social media, I recommend that you install monitoring software or apps on the devices your child uses. They offer a built-in accountability, especially if they know you are receiving reports of their activity.

Remember, you are the parent, and you have the right to change, adjust, or even abolish privileges along the way. Smartphones and social media have changed the landscape of relationships and many young people are more content to hang out in groups virtually rather than pair up as couples. While this is certainly good news, it also presents some new challenges in that it has left adolescents emboldened behind their screens to explore opposite sex relationships (or for that matter, same-sex relationships) with little to no adult supervision at a time when they lack emotional maturity and confidence in their God-given identity and sense of worth.

High School: The Training Ground

If ever you need to be extra attentive to your daughter's level of interest in boys, it's during her high school years. Honestly, this is the season of life where her dating attitudes will be molded. If you have not begun to lay the groundwork for what you deem to be acceptable and unacceptable, she will get her cues from the culture at large. Having witnessed so many female casualties in my ministry to girls, I walked into my daughter's high school years loaded for bear and ready to fight for a better standard. Of course, I was up against the challenge of finding that tricky balance where you draw firm boundaries yet, at the same time, allow for a little breathing room so she doesn't grow exasperated and stage an all-out rebellion. Below are some rules we put in place on the front end of her high school experience and a brief explanation of the *why* behind each one:

- I told my daughter that she would not be allowed to date or go out with a boy prior to her junior year, and at that point we would evaluate the situation (should there be a suitor) on a case-by-case basis. Why this rule? I cannot think of a single case in all my years of ministry to girls where a serious dating relationship during the early years of high school produced, overall, positive results.

Maybe exceptions can be found, but I am not aware of a single one. Most girls are not emotionally, physically, or spiritually prepared to handle the responsibility and drama that comes with an exclusive dating relationship. Not to mention, you are playing Russian roulette with her purity when you allow the dating process to begin at such an early age. I have watched good Christian girls fall like flies in their high school years because they thought they were strong enough to have a serious boyfriend and follow Jesus at the same time. By drawing a firm line in the sand on the front end, my daughter knew it wasn't up for debate and, therefore, concentrated on hanging out with male friends, as well as building her female friendships.

- Once my daughter was allowed to date or go out with someone, my husband set aside a time to meet with the young man to make him aware of our rules, curfews, and expectations in the relationship. In doing this, we knew that it would require our daughter to be more thoughtful and selective when it came to the character of the young man in question. In other words, many guys would cut and run upon hearing about this requirement. Good riddance, I say. If he truly cares about our daughter, he will stick around and rise to the level of our expectations.

- While under our roof, an approved dating relationship will never be allowed to escalate to the "joined at the hip" status that is all too common in the high school years. Other than the obvious fact that the more time a couple spends together one-on-one, the more likely they will eventually succumb to physical temptations, it also deters from quality time spent with family, friends, and, most importantly, God.

- We emphasized to our daughter that she should consider only dating Christians. The truth is, you marry someone you date, so dating someone who is not a Christian is not worth the gamble. If he doesn't share the same values and beliefs, the relationship isn't worth pursuing. Period. End of sentence. Run fast and run far. Dating should never be a mission field. There's too much at stake to risk it. Oftentimes it backfires, and the Christian ends up relaxing her values in an effort to make the relationship work.

- Long before my daughter had her first official boyfriend, I told her to prepare and practice her speech detailing her physical boundaries and told her that it wasn't a matter of *if* she needed the speech but *when*. Knowing your boundaries is especially important that a recent survey found that a quarter of young people (twelve to twenty) felt pressuring someone into sex was normal.[1] The survey results concluded that "violation of girls' boundaries is so prevalent and starts so young that it can come to seem normal."[2] All the more reason we must be diligent in teaching our daughters the importance of adopting boundaries as well as knowing how to verbalize their boundaries in sensitive situations.

How did this new and revised definition of dating work out, you might wonder? My daughter did not experience a dating relationship until the second semester of her senior year of high school. I am ever so grateful for the delay in that it enabled her to gain some maturity along the way. By the time she began to date, she had witnessed the fallout many of her friends suffered from their own dating experiences and taken note of their heartaches. One added advantage I had in my corner that delayed the dating process was that my daughter was a late bloomer. While this was at times frustrating for her, I was counting my blessings that the boys were paying more attention to the girls who, let's just say, were looking more like young women than little girls.

If your daughter is showing signs of early development, just a heads-up that you could face a bigger challenge when it comes to keeping the boys at bay and your daughter disinterested. It is difficult to push the pause button in the rush to grow up when your daughter is already wearing your same bra size . . . or bigger. Girls who develop at an earlier age are often noticed by the older boys as well as treated the age they look rather than the age they are. As a mother, you will have to work overtime to minimize this effect. And certainly, don't encourage the attention. I have always been amazed at the mothers who brag about the male attention their daughters receive for being more developed.

Reminding Your Daughter of "Whose" She Is

In my years of working with teen and college girls, I have had a fair share cry on my shoulder over actions that left them with tainted reputations. Because of a lack of frontal lobe development in the tween and teen years, it is difficult for our daughters to mentally walk a decision down its logical path and weigh the possible consequences of the action in question. Most of us likely can relate to that challenge during our adolescent and teen years and have our own fair share of negative consequences we tallied up as a result. However, this is where we must be faithful in helping our daughters see that actions determine character and character, in turn, determines reputation.

Proverbs 22:1 reminds us that "a good name is more desirable than great riches." Socrates, the Greek philosopher from the fourth century BC, once said, "Regard your good name as the richest jewel that can possibly be possessed. The way to gain a good reputation is to endeavor to be what you desire to appear." Girls who are diligently taught that they were created in the image of God and encouraged to define their worth according to who they are in Christ as opposed to the shallow standards of the culture, will endeavor to become the person they see through God's eyes. Further, they are not willing to compromise their identity, worth, or value by engaging in any behavior that would seek to dishonor who (or better yet, Whose) they are.

We must be faithful in sharing the key to obtaining a good reputation with our daughters. *What is the key?* you may wonder. It can be found in Proverbs 3:1–4: "My son, do not forget my teaching, but keep my commands in your heart, for they will prolong your life many years and bring you prosperity. Let love and faithfulness never leave you; bind them around your neck, write them on the tablet of your heart. Then you will win favor and a good name in the sight of God and man." In order to remember God's teaching, our daughters must first know God's teaching. Upon knowing it, they must tuck it away in their hearts and pull from that reserve when the need arises. This is the point of impact when God's standard goes beyond a simple head knowledge and takes root in the heart. We can do our part to provide them with adequate teaching over the years, but we cannot make them treasure that teaching in their hearts. It will have to be up to them to believe it. Our job is to do what we can to teach them God's principles and protect their hearts to the best of our abilities. Most importantly, we must never cease to pray for our daughters.

An Umbrella of Protection

In *The Body Project*, author Joan Jacobs Brumberg makes the thoughtful observation that "most Americans came to believe that a hallmark of Christian civilization was its ability to nurture and protect girlhood innocence: in effect, to guarantee a safe time between menarche and marriage, when girls would be sexually inactive. This principle influenced Victorian mothers in their dealings with developing daughters, and it animated countless community efforts to monitor and supervise young women in single-sex groups designed to promote innocence and purity."[3] Let's not forget that fifty years ago young women typically went through puberty later and married earlier. In addition, there were stricter standards of dating and courtship during this time period, and it was common for parents to chaperone their children's coed activities.

Recently, I was reading an etiquette book that dates back to 1956, which I picked up in an antique store. In a chapter on manners, it addressed "conventions for the single woman living alone." Here is what it said: "There used to be only two conventionally acceptable ways for a marriageable young woman to live apart from her relatives: one was to live with a family who were friends of her parents, the other was to set up housekeeping in a respectable apartment house, complete with doorman, under the surveillance of an elderly servant chosen by her mother."[4] In times past, parents were intentional about providing a safe umbrella of protection over their daughter until she had transitioned into marriage.

We are not excused today from providing our daughters with a new and updated "umbrella of protection" during the all too fleeting season of girlhood. As part of this effort, my husband and I took a few extra steps to provide additional protection for our daughter in her dating experiences. In addition to her dad having a talk with her first boyfriend (late high school), I also called and introduced myself to his mother. In the course of the conversation, I shared that one of the rules we feel strongly about is that our daughter not spend time at this young man's house without a parent present (and our permission beforehand). We had the same rule for times when they were here in our home, and once we went upstairs to bed, he had to leave. In addition, we required that the young man come over to the house to pick her up even when they were planning to spend time at his house. At first our daughter balked a bit at this requirement, but we explained that a little chivalry goes a long way. While we didn't expect him to break the bank taking her out on formal dates each time they got together, we did expect that he treat their informal get-togethers with the same level of respect. By keeping the lines of communication open, it sent the message that her father and I would be engaged in the process.

When I think about the responsibility of parents to provide an umbrella of protection over our daughters in regard to opposite sex relationships, I am reminded of Proverbs 4:23. We are helping them learn to "guard their hearts." In the book *Raising Girls*, authors Melissa Trevathan and Sissy Goff address the balance of "gradually introducing your daughter into the world of boys" and while at the same time allowing her "enough freedom at home to be able to learn to make wise decisions regarding boys so that when she leaves home she can take that wisdom with her."[5] They note that "if a girl has no prior experience with boys, casual or otherwise, this danger can be compounded" when she leaves home. The authors also echo my belief that "it is helpful for her to have already had practice in this kind of decision making while she still lives under your roof," noting that "the best time for girls to make mistakes is while they are at home." They offer further wisdom in saying, "As she grows up, you can gradually widen the boundaries—giving her room to make her own decisions within the care of your watchful eye."[6] If we are having necessary conversations along the way with our daughters that outline a parent-approved model of dating, hopefully they will carry that same model and mind-set with them when they leave. Even for the girls who are not presented with an opportunity to date in the high school years, our words will not be wasted. We will have, at least, provided a framework for when the dating opportunity presents itself in God's timing.

In the case of my daughter, her short high school dating experience proved to be a valuable training ground for her to develop a healthier dating mind-set to carry into her college years. By then, she had gained confidence in her own dating standards and had the needed maturity to maintain her commitment to hold out for God's best. She had one boyfriend in college and she ended up marrying him in her senior year. My husband and I could not have handpicked a better spouse for her. He possesses a godly maturity far beyond his years and faithfully loves our daughter "as Christ loved the church" (Eph. 5:25).

On the night before our daughter's wedding, her father presented her with a locket at the rehearsal dinner that contained a small picture of her and her soon-to-be husband. It hung on a gold chain next to a locket my husband had given our daughter when she was four years old that contained a picture of Paige and her daddy. As Paige stood between her father and Matt, my husband shared that he had given her that first locket on an ice cream date as a symbol of a promise that as her father, he would help her protect her heart until she was ready to give it away. On that night before her wedding, he proudly handed the reins of responsibility over to her soon-to-be husband Matt. Of course, there wasn't a dry eye in the house. It was a beautiful picture of the prize that awaits those who learn to guard their hearts. As parents, it's up to us to show them how.

Talk about It

· · · · · · · · · · ·

Chapter 4

Were you aware of the link between excessive screen time and mental health? After reading the data, what changes do you feel led to make when it comes to your daughter's access to screens?

How have screens impacted your daughter's behavior overall? Is she able to manage her screen time in moderation or does she have a tendency to over-indulge?

Would you agree that much of our compulsion toward screens (and other distractions) is rooted in a fear of solitude? How might you teach your daughter that solitude is a good thing and necessary if she is to have a close, thriving relationship with Christ?

What changes might you need to make regarding technology if you were to ask yourself on a consistent basis, "Is this good for my soul?" What about your daughter?

Chapter 5

Have you experienced the awkward transition of your daughter gravitating away from you, and toward her friends or peer group? If so, describe how it left you feeling at the time.

List your daughter's friends who would qualify as "weekend friends." What about "weekday friends"?

Does your daughter have any "high-risk friends"? If she has more than one or two, what steps can you take to help encourage her to find friends who share your same values?

In your opinion, how has technology/social media changed the friendship dynamic as compared to when you were growing up?

Chapter 6

Assuming your daughter is old enough, has she shown an interest at any level in boys? How did you respond?

If/when she is old enough to date or "go out," what rules or boundaries do/will you have in place?

Do you feel your daughter has a good grasp on "whose she is" or does she define her worth based on the attention she gets from boys?

What steps are you taking to provide an "umbrella of protection" to help your daughter protect her heart when it comes to boys and dating?

Conversation 3

Have a little sex respect.

Chapter 7

Beyond the Birds and Bees

● ● ● ● ● ●

"The body, however, is not meant for sexual immorality but for the Lord, and the Lord for the body." (1 Cor. 6:13)

I have a friend who, when her kids were young, insisted on referring to their private parts by the correct anatomical terms, while I, on the other hand, provided my children with nicknames. She would tease me about it often and tell me that I was going to mess them up for life. My little nickname system worked just fine until one day when a new family moved into our neighborhood. I had heard that they also had a six-year-old boy, the same age as my oldest at the time, so we stopped by one day to introduce ourselves. When the mother introduced her son to my son, Ryan, I immediately knew we had a problem. Unfortunately, he shared the same name as um, well, you know—I still can't say it! Anyway, I shot my son a pleading look to remain silent, but by the look on his face, I knew we would have plenty to talk about on the way home. I'll never forget his comment as we walked away: "Mom, why would anyone name their kid Willy?" Drats. I would have to come clean and just in time, mind you. The movie *Free Willy* released the following year. It's a good thing we cleared the matter up.

If I thought the anatomy conversation was stressful, it was nothing compared to the conversations that would follow in years to come about sex. Of course, every generation of parents wonders when to broach the topic of sex, what to say, and more importantly, how much to say. The goal is to educate our children with the facts about sex through a biblical lens before they are educated by the culture, their peers, or worse yet, the Internet. There is too much at risk to remain silent on the topic or for that matter, show up late to the game. Given the times, our children are being exposed at younger ages than ever before to sexual themes and misinformation about sex. Even if you are vigilant when it comes to guarding your child's innocence, you can't adequately monitor the outside influences that may expose your child to the topic of sex long before they are emotionally ready to process the information (or rather, misinformation).

I recently read an article in a vintage *Parents' Magazine* from 1938 entitled "Then and Now" where parents were given a similar charge to take the initiative to discuss the topic of sex with their children before their children were educated elsewhere.[1] Nowhere are the changes in attitude more striking than in that department of parent education having to do with what used to be called "imparting the facts of life." Relying on journals and other parenting sources dating back a hundred years prior, the article compares the "then" attitudes of parents in the early 1800s regarding how they addressed the topic of sex to the "now" attitudes in the 1930's. Parents in the early 1800s were advised, "Before nine, children are not very curious and can be put off without a definite answer about birth. When it is impossible to avoid answering, they can be told that the doctor brought the baby, so that they would not be told an untruth, and would be satisfied for the time being. When children reach the age of nine or ten they should be told the truth by parents in such a way that they will be impressed with the beauty and wonder of nature. They can be told without mentioning anything of sex relations. Children are usually satisfied with this, up to the age of fourteen or fifteen years." Fourteen or fifteen years and no mention of "sex relations" is necessary? Perhaps, this is where the folklore of the stork delivering babies originated!

The article follows with the advice offered to parents in the 1930s, nearly a century later. "We know now that we must come closer to the realities with our children, answering not what they ask but what they really want to know about life as they read of it in the daily press, hear of it on the radio, see it in the movies. By the time they are fourteen or fifteen, they are usually telling us." If only our biggest worry regarding early exposure was that our children might hear mention of sex on the radio, or see hints of it on a movie that would likely have garnered a PG-13 rating in our culture today. Today's parents have to accept the sad reality that try as we may, we will not be able to shield our children from early exposure to sex that has become so pervasive in our culture. Even if they are not seeking it out, chances are, it will find them. Just recently, a friend of mine who teaches second graders shared that she overheard some of the boys telling the girls about sex and asking them if they wanted "to do it." Seven- and eight-year-olds.

When we are talking with our children about sex, we need to approach the topic with boldness and confidence rather than skittishness and timidity. We also need to make sure we are balanced in the way we present it, always remembering that sex was created by God, for His purposes (procreation) and our pleasure. In other words, we need to leave our daughters with a clear understanding that sex in the right context (marriage) is good and something God wired us to desire and enjoy. In the book *Hooked*, authors Joe S. McIlhaney, M.D., and Freda McKissic Bush, M.D., say, "Sex can be considered one of the appetites with which we are born."[2] They go on to point out that the word "appetite" can be defined as "any of the instinctive desires necessary to keep up organic life" or "an inherent craving."[3] McIlhaney and Bush say, "A truth to remember is that appetites are necessary, but values-neutral. They can be used appropriately or they can be misunderstood and misused. For example, without an appetite for food, we wouldn't survive. Food provides energy and fuels our bodies. Yet the misuse of this natural appetite in the forms of overeating or eating too much of the wrong things, can cause problems such as cardiovascular disease, diabetes, and many other issues. These health problems can dramatically change the entire course of an individual's life."[4]

As mothers, we need to be careful that we don't go overboard in our conversations by always emphasizing the problems associated with sex outside of marriage. If we fail to acknowledge that sex is, in fact, a gift from God and something He gave us a natural appetite for, our daughters may be left with the impression that sex is shameful, even in marriage. This will be especially confusing for our daughters when sexual curiosity kicks in (and it will!). We need to make sure our daughters understand that it is perfectly normal to have a desire to experience sex or engage in sexual activity, but that desire needs to be properly managed in order for them to experience optimum long-term spiritual, emotional, and physical health.

The Truth about Saving Sex for Marriage

If we needed any more proof that our children are growing up in a post-Christian culture, look no further than attitudes regarding sex outside of marriage. In her book iGen, author Jean Twenge notes, "As late as 2006, about 50 percent of eighteen–twenty-nine-year-olds believed that sex between two unmarried adults was 'not wrong at all'—about the same as in the 1970's. Then approval of premarital sex shot upward, with 65 percent of young people in 2016 declaring it 'not wrong at all.' Even sex between young teens (those sixteen or younger) became more accepted, with five times as many declaring it 'not wrong at all' in 2016 than in 1986. iGen'ers are just less willing to label anything as 'wrong'—it's all up to the individual."[5] She goes on to say that with the average age of marriage rising to the late twenties, "iGen'ers may find the idea of waiting until they get married to be ridiculous."[6]

Studies show that girls are developing earlier than ever before and with that early development comes hormones. Couple that with the delay in marriage (the average age for women is twenty-seven) and you see the challenge we face. A hundred years ago, remaining sexually pure until marriage, for the average girl, meant exercising self-control for four to six years. Today, for the average girl, delaying sex means exercising self-control for ten to fourteen years.

As Christian mothers, we often tell our girls to remain pure while at the same time encouraging them to delay marriage and enjoy being single. I will address attitudes regarding the popular mind-set that marriage should be delayed in the next conversation, but for the sake of this conversation, it is necessary to question whether this is an unrealistic expectation to place on our daughters. They can hardly escape the culture's empowerment message that encourages them to climb the career ladder before considering marriage and motherhood, but are we also playing a part in making it difficult for our daughters to maintain their purity by peddling the same message?

Another factor that needs to be considered before beginning "the talk" is the finding that for adolescents there is a lag between the body's capability and the mind's capacity to comprehend the consequences of sex.[7] Let me sum that up for you: When we tell our teen-aged daughters, "If you have sex before you're married, you could get pregnant," their brains are not cognitively developed enough to walk down a worst-case scenario path and consider the full weight of incurable STDs or teen pregnancy. Their bodies are saying "do it," and their brains have not caught up to say, "If you do, you might get pregnant and find yourself up in the middle of the night with a colicky infant while your friends are at the senior prom." Nor are they able to see past the moment of desired pleasure to weigh the long-term consequences of STDs, abortion, or compromised mental and spiritual health.

Another study related to the lag in cognitive development when it comes to adolescent reasoning concluded that "teenagers need 'practice at recognizing cues in the environment that signal possible danger before it's too late to act.'"[8] Therefore, it is critical to teach our daughters to recognize when they are in over their heads regarding sexual temptation. Stop for a minute and think about the biblical counsel we give them to "flee temptation." How often do we go a step further and give them practical ways to flee or the words to say when they find themselves in a precarious situation?

In my ministry to teen girls, I encountered countless young women who said they went too far sexually because they didn't know what to say in the situation. Again, this may sound absurd to those of us who are adults and are better equipped to put our thoughts into words, but for an adolescent teen with raging hormones and little ability to think on her feet, it's a real and present problem. For example, when discussing this with my own daughter, I encouraged her to come up with actual verbiage of what she might say when faced with a sexually tempting situation, and as ridiculous as it may sound, practice her lines in front of her bathroom mirror to get them down pat.

Valerie F. Reyna, professor of human development and psychology at the New York State College of Human Ecology at Cornell and an author of the study, also cautions: "Younger adolescents don't learn from consequences as well as older adolescents do. So rather than relying on them to make reasoned choices or to learn from the school of hard knocks, a better approach is to supervise them. . . . A young teenage girl should not be left alone in the house with her boyfriend, and responsible adults should be omnipresent and alcohol absent when teenagers have parties."[9]

In summary, parents should draw firm boundaries and behave like parents. If our kids are unable to assess all the risks associated with an action, we essentially step in and protect them from themselves. One of my son's college-aged friends shared candidly with me that he had ended a relationship with his Christian girlfriend of more than three years in an effort to maintain sexual purity after having gone too far in the relationship. He mentioned that part of their temptation was a lack of rules or boundaries on the part of her parents when he was at her home. Mind you, these are Christian parents. He shared that even while dating in high school, it was not uncommon to be left alone in the house while her parents were gone. In other words, he was stunned and amazed that her parents trusted them as much as they did! He ended his comments with the conclusion, "When I have kids. . . !"

What can we learn from this information regarding the lag in cognitive development? Dr. Reyna stated that as people grow older and more experienced, they became more intuitive, and more of their decisions are based on an overall sense of what is the best course of action. And who better than their mother to help guide kids to the best course of action and teach them to look to God for "intuition," all the while, providing plenty of rules and supervision along the way.

Unless we expose the faulty thinking behind the culture's free-sex message and the fallout that has resulted from believing it, it will be impossible to adequately address the issue of sex outside of marriage with our daughters. It's not enough to tell our daughters to "wait because God says so." They deserve to know all the facts before making a decision to have sex outside of marriage. Our daughters are not being told the truth about the fallout related to sex outside of marriage; therefore, it's up to us to inform them.

Perhaps one of the most ironic factors regarding the culture's message that girls should pursue sexual freedom is that almost half (41 percent) of girls ages fourteen to seventeen reported having "unwanted sex" because they feared their partner would get angry if denied sex.[10] Another study found that even when the sex is wanted, it is often soon regretted. In fact, the National Campaign to Prevent Teen Pregnancy found that two-thirds of all sexually experienced teens said that they wished they had waited longer before having sex.[11]

Dawn Eden, author of the book *The Thrill of the Chaste: Finding Fulfillment While Keeping Your Clothes On*, admits that her pursuit of sexual freedom left her feeling anything but free. She confessed, "When I sought sexual experiences with men, it was as a distraction from the emptiness I felt inside."[12] The more I examine the mounting evidence that sex outside of marriage has a negative impact on the physical, emotional, and spiritual development of young women, the more I understand God's wisdom in 1 Corinthians 6:13: "The body is not meant for sexual immorality, but for the Lord, and the Lord for the body" (ESV).

Christian Kids Are Having Sex Too

According to the Center for Disease Control and Prevention, American women, on average, first have intercourse at 17.2 years old. The most recent available data shows that as of 2013, 89.1 percent of married women had engaged in premarital sex.[13] Nationwide, 41.2 percent of students had had sexual intercourse.[14] But what about our Christian kids? In theory, 80 percent of "evangelical" or "born again" teenagers think sex should be saved for marriage. Unfortunately, there appears to be a huge disconnect when it comes to walking the talk. According to a study, *Forbidden Fruit: Sex & Religion in the Lives of American Teenagers* by Mark Regnerus, a professor of sociology at the University of Texas at Austin, evangelical teens are actually more likely to have lost their virginity than either mainline Protestants or Catholics, and they lose their virginity at a slightly younger age—16.3, as compared to 16.7 for mainline Protestants and Catholics. In addition, they are much more likely to have had three or more sexual partners by age seventeen (13.7 percent of evangelicals versus 8.9 percent for mainline Protestants).[15]

Equally disturbing, evangelical teens scored low on a quiz related to pregnancy and health risks. The authors of the study speculate that parents of "evangelical teens" may be talking to their kids about sex, but the conversation is more focused on the morals rather than the mechanics. In other words, we seem to have the "don't do it until your married" part down but stop short of giving them advice based on a hypothetical "but if you do decide to have sex . . ." (And over 90 percent will.) The article further states, "Evangelical teens don't accept themselves as people who will have sex until they've already had it."[16]

Therein lies the problem. If they don't *expect* to have sex, they aren't *prepared* to have sex. And if we don't expect them to have sex, we don't leave them prepared should they succumb to the temptation and have sex. In fact, half of all mothers of sexually active teenagers mistakenly believe their children are still virgins, according to a team of researchers at the University of Minnesota Adolescent Health Center.[17]

Regnerus sums up our ignorance to the problem well. "For evangelicals, sex is a 'symbolic boundary' marking a good Christian from a bad one, but in reality, the kids are always 'sneaking across enemy lines.'"[18] That is a humbling thought for well-meaning Christian parents who can also relate to sneaking across enemy lines in their own teen years. When you mix the culture's message, that sex is natural, with the hormone factor, there is little to hold them back. Nowadays a girl is considered fairly exceptional if she can make it to her wedding day with less than three sexual partners or commit herself to secondary virginity at some point. I've even heard of a trend among couples to abstain from sex for a brief time before the wedding in an attempt to make it more special. Is this as good as it gets?

God knew what He was doing when He created sex for the confines of marriage. It's up to us to educate our daughters to the why behind His rules. No doubt we have our work cut out for us. We must have some candid and blunt conversations with our daughters to arm them in the battle they face.

The Benefits of Waiting

In addition to ignoring the fallout from having sex outside of marriage, the media also fails to address the benefits of saving sex for marriage. Think about it. When was the last time you heard a media report announcing that those who abstain from sex outside of marriage have the best sex once they are married? One survey where eleven hundred people were asked about their sexual satisfaction found that 72 percent of all married "traditionalists" (those who "strongly believe out of wedlock sex is wrong") reported a higher sexual satisfaction. "Traditionalists" scored roughly thirty-one percentage points higher than the level registered by unmarried "nontraditionalists" (those who have no or only some objection to sex outside of marriage) and thirteen percentage points higher than married nontraditionalists.[19] Another study by the National Institute for Healthcare Research found that couples who don't sleep together before marriage and who are faithful during marriage are more satisfied with their current sex life and also with their marriages compared to those who were involved sexually before marriage.[20]

And the perks don't stop there. Several researchers with the Heritage Foundation analyzed data from the 1995 National Survey of Family Growth and found that for women thirty or older, those who were monogamous (only one sexual partner in a lifetime) were by far most likely to be still in a stable relationship (80 percent). Sleeping with just one extra partner dropped that probability to 54 percent. Two extra partners brought it down to 44 percent.[21] Clearly, there is a link between self-restraint practiced before marriage and a lasting and fruitful marriage. Most of our girls would admit to wanting a healthy and happy marriage as a long-term goal. I wonder how many might alter their behavior and choose to abstain if they knew that, in doing so, they would greatly increase their likelihood of remaining in a lasting, monogamous marriage.

Let me put this into perspective. Here is the exact conversation I had with my own daughter to illustrate this powerful finding. "Paige, if you line up ten of your friends who have already had two or more sexual partners, approximately six will be divorced by their twentieth high school reunion. However, if you line up ten girls who successfully abstain from sex prior to marriage (of which I hope you will be one), only two will be divorced by their twentieth high school reunion. In other words, if you sleep with just two guys prior to marriage, you will be three times more likely to divorce than if you abstain."[22] The decision to have sex outside of marriage can literally be a predictor of future happiness in a young woman's life.

Of course, you don't hear the media highlighting any of the above data. The culture will continue to tell our daughters that sex outside of marriage is a natural, normal part of life. It is imperative that we as mothers pick up the slack and share with our daughters the benefits of sexual purity that the culture refuses to address. We owe it to our daughters to tell them the truth—the *whole* truth.

Sex Education through the Years

In the next chapter, we will be discussing the greatest risks our daughters will face when it comes to sex and sexual activity. Be warned that the next couple of chapters may leave you feeling overwhelmed with the challenge we face. It's important to remember that none of this has caught God off guard. His principles and truths have stood the test of time, and He has given us everything we need to pass His truths along to our children.

I found some wonderful tips from the Mayo Clinic offered on their site. They break it down according to age and level of understanding.[23]

Age 18 Months–3 Years

Children begin to learn about their own bodies. Teach your child the proper names for sex organs. Otherwise, he or she might get the idea that something is wrong with these parts of the body.

Ages 3–4 Years

Take advantage of everyday opportunities to discuss sex. If there's a pregnancy in the family, for example, tell your children that babies grow in a special place inside the mother. If your children want more details on how the baby got there or how the baby will be born, offer them.

Consider these examples:

* How do babies get inside a mommy's tummy? You might say: "A mom and a dad make a baby by holding each other in a special way."

- How are babies born? For some kids, it might be enough to say, "Doctors and nurses help babies who are ready to be born."
- Where do babies come from? Try to give a simple and direct response, such as: "Babies grow in a special place inside the mother." As your child matures, you can add more details.

Teach your child that the parts of the body covered by a bathing suit are private and that no one should be allowed to touch them without permission.

Ages 5–7 Years

Questions about sex will become more complex as your child tries to understand the connection between sexuality and making babies. He or she may turn to friends for some of these answers. Because children can pick up faulty information about sex and reproduction, it may be best to ask what your child knows about a particular topic before you start explaining it.

Ages 8–12 Years

Children between the ages of eight and twelve worry a lot about whether they are "normal." Children of the same age mature at wildly different rates. Reassure your child that he or she is well within the normal range of development.

Ages 13+ Years

The American Academy of Pediatrics recommends that before they reach puberty children should have a basic understanding of:

- The names and functions of male and female sex organs

- What happens during puberty and what the physical changes of puberty mean—movement into young womanhood or young manhood
- The nature and purpose of the menstrual cycle
- What sexual intercourse is and how females become pregnant
- How to prevent pregnancy
- Same-sex relationships
- Masturbation
- Activities that spread sexually transmitted diseases (STDs), in particular AIDS
- Your expectations and values[24]

Be honest, open, and matter-of-fact. Talking about sexual matters with your child can make you both feel uncomfortable and embarrassed. Let your child guide the talk with his or her questions. Don't giggle or laugh, even if the question is cute. Try not to appear overly embarrassed or serious. If you have been open with your child's questions since the beginning, your child will more likely come to you with his or her questions in the future. The best place for your child to learn about relationships, love, commitment, and respect is from you.[25]

While the list above ends with ages thirteen and above, I feel it's necessary to also add an additional conversation for those who save sex for their wedding night. Years ago, a young coworker was just weeks away from her wedding and shared with me that she was afraid to have sex and not sure what to expect. She was raised in a Christian home and attended a private Christian school, and she confessed that her mother had never once broached the topic of sex. Mothers, she is not alone. Over the years of serving in ministry to girls, I have heard from other young women who have saved themselves for their wedding night and express a similar fear over what to expect. Knowing this, led me to have many conversations with my daughter after she was engaged to her now husband. They had both managed to save themselves for their wedding night and I candidly told her that first-time sex is not usually enjoyable. I told her it could be awkward, painful, and possibly even unsuccessful, but to hang in there because it gets better. A lot better. I went on to tell her, "What better person to enjoy all that awkwardness with than your husband?!"

Regardless of the age or stage of your child, addressing the topic of sex should not be a daunting task nor should it be shrouded in shame or secrecy. If we truly view sex as a beautiful gift from God to be enjoyed in the sanctity of marriage, it should be treated no differently than other God-given appetite we openly talk about with our children. The culture has robbed sex of its dignity and beauty and it's up to us to educate our children as to God's true intent for sex.

Chapter 8

Play Now, Pay Later

● ● ● ● ● ●

Flee from sexual immorality. Every other sin a person commits is outside the body, but the sexually immoral person sins against his own body. (1 Cor. 6:18 ESV)

Your daughter is bombarded with messages regarding sex on a daily basis. The general message to women is that sex is a symbol of empowerment, signifying strength and independence. Unfortunately, our girls are not being told the whole story. When was the last time you saw a scene on TV or in a movie that, after highlighting sex outside of marriage, showed one of the characters dealing with an unwanted pregnancy? Or what about the aftermath of abortion where depression and regret are commonly experienced? What if the media reflected the reality that one-fourth of all teen girls has an STD and allowed one-fourth of their female characters to contract an STD? What if the media portrayed the fallout from contracting an STD—like working up your nerve to tell your partner or, for that matter, your future partners? Or what if they pulled back the curtain and showed the devastating fallout that often occurs when a young woman caves in and sends a nude picture to her boyfriend only to have it shared with others in the aftermath of a breakup?

Of course, our girls won't see reality because it doesn't line up with the empowerment message the culture is preaching. So the lie continues to be peddled day in and day out, leaving our girls with the impression that sex is nothing more than a recreational hobby. No consequences, no strings attached. But there *are* consequences, and there *are* strings attached, but no one has the guts to say it. The real paradox is that, in the end, sexual freedom often leaves our young women physically, emotionally, and spiritually entangled in a mess of fallout. And when one is entangled, they are hardly free.

The Truth about Hooking Up

First, the good news. Sexual intercourse among teens is on the decline. Some experts speculate this is due to the fact that so much of their social time is spent online and as a result, they spend less time with their peers in person. One college woman offered another explanation on the decline of teen sex. "Teens are being scared into not having sex. When I was in high school the 'no sex' propaganda was strong. We watched videos of what diseased genitals looked like, and we heard all the stories about teen moms. The show *Teen Mom* came out, and nobody wanted to be those girls. Their lives were sad and pathetic."[1]

However, before you begin to celebrate, there is also speculation that the decline in teen sexual intercourse is due to an increase in oral sex. When Peggy Orenstein, author of the book *Girls & Sex*, interviewed teen girls, several described oral sex as "nothing . . . it's not sex" and "a step past making out with someone." Some argued it was safer and "doesn't have the repercussions that vaginal sex does. You're not losing your virginity, you can't get pregnant, you can't get STDs. So it's safer."[2] Of course, we know this is not true since you can get STDs from oral sex.

While the decline in sexual intercourse among teens is worth celebrating, we cannot minimize the impact many other behaviors are having on our girls when it comes to sexual activity. While we often label teen pregnancy as the most devastating outcome of unprotected sex, there are many others that are producing life-altering consequences. Take for example, hooking up. Many moms naively postpone discussing the topic of sex until their daughters are in a dating relationship. The problem with that is that dating is nearly extinct. One multi-year survey of more than twenty-four thousand college students from twenty-two different US colleges and universities found that just as many students are hooking up as are dating. Sixty-two percent reported having hooked up since the beginning of their college experience, while 61 percent reported going out on a date.[3]

When it comes to hooking up, the rules of the game are pretty simple: "Sex is okay as long as it's mutual and protected; so go for it!" Hooking up gained traction among many feminists who were outraged that women were so sexually repressed (translation: sex was only accepted in marriage) and began to rally for the same perks typically enjoyed by men: sex on demand with no strings attached. And here we are today, some fifty-plus years later, and they have their wish. The men, of course, were more than happy to oblige the women in their quest for sexual liberation, and today we are experiencing the fruits of the sexual revolution. The only problem is that the fruit is rotten. But in spite of this obvious evidence, the free sex message continues to thrive; in fact, it is only getting worse.

A separate study sponsored by the Independent Women's Forum called "Hooking Up, Hanging Out, and Hoping for Mr. Right" further proved that our free sex culture is not without heavy emotional consequences. The study found an alarming trend of young people hooking up for casual sex without any promise of commitment or long-term relationships. The report was based on surveys of college women who all but confirmed that traditional dating is a thing of the past. The independence and empowerment promised to women by the sexual revolution as a result of no-commitment hookups has left young women feeling anything but empowered. In fact, 61 percent of survey respondents said that a hookup makes them feel "desirable" but also "awkward."[4] Here is further proof that it is nearly impossible to detach yourself emotionally from the physical act of sex. One Princeton grad summed it up this way: "The whole thing is a very male-dominated scene. Hooking up lets men get physical pleasure without any emotional connection, but for the women it's hard to separate the physical from the emotional. Women want the call the next day."[5]

Oxytocin: The Bonding Hormone

There is a valid reason women want the call the next day. God has wired their brains to connect sex with intimacy and trust. The kind of intimacy and trust reserved for marriage and science backs this theory up. Neuroscientists have discovered a chemical that is involved in the bonding process called oxytocin. Oxytocin is a hormone that acts as a messenger from one organ to another and has been linked as the hormone that is sent from the brain to the uterus and breasts to induce labor, as well as to let down milk after the baby is born. But here's where it gets interesting. It has been discovered that oxytocin is also released during sexual activity.[6] Author of *Unprotected: A Campus Psychiatrist Reveals How Political Correctness in Her Profession Endangers Every Student*, Anonymous, M.D, asks, "Could it be that the same chemical that flows through a woman's veins as she nurses her infant, promoting a powerful and selfless devotion is found in college women 'hooking up' with men whose last intention is to bond?"[7] Interestingly, it has also been discovered that in addition to bonding, oxytocin increases trust.[8] Trust, no doubt, intended between a newborn and a mother or a husband and wife.

Psychologist Jess Lair, of Montana State University, describes the bonding process that takes place during sexual intercourse in this way: "Sexual bonding includes powerful emotional, psychological, physical, and spiritual links that are so strong that the two people become one, at least for a moment. Sexual intercourse is an intense, though brief physical bonding that leaves indelible marks on the participants. . . . To believe one can walk away from a sexual experience untouched is dangerously naïve."[9]

Perhaps this is why Jesus instructed, "For this reason a man will leave his father and mother and be united to his wife, and the two will become one flesh.' So they are no longer two, but one flesh" (Mark 10:7–8). And the apostle Paul warned: "Do you not know that your bodies are members of Christ himself? Shall I then take the members of Christ and unite them with a prostitute? Never! Do you not know that he who unites himself with a prostitute is one with her in body? For it is said, 'The two will become one flesh.' But whoever is united with the Lord is one with him in spirit" (1 Cor. 6:15–17). Should we be surprised that science discovering actual evidence to support what God has been telling us all along—that sex was created by Him for the purpose of forging an intimate bond of trust between husband and wife? Further, should we be surprised that when sex is engaged in outside of the intimacy and trust of a marriage relationship, it will result in an emptiness because it wasn't created to be a casual recreation?

Dawn Eden in *The Thrill of the Chaste* describes the conflict of emotions that occurs after casual sex that lends support to the oxytocin research. She says:

> When I was having casual sex, there was one moment I dreaded more than any other. I dreaded it not out of fear that the sex would be bad, but out of fear that it would be good. If the sex was good, then, even if I knew in my heart that the relationship wouldn't work, I would still feel as though the act had bonded me with my sex partner in a deeper way than we had been bonded before. It's in the nature of sex to awaken deep emotions within us— emotions that are distinctly unwelcome when one is trying to keep it light. At such times, the worst moment was when it was all over. Suddenly, I was jarred back to earth. Then I'd lie back and feel . . . bereft. My partner was still there, and if I was really lucky, he'd lie down next to me. Yet, I couldn't help feeling like the spell had been broken. We could nuzzle or giggle, or we could fall asleep in each other's arms, but I knew I was playacting—and so did my partner. We weren't really intimate—it had just been a game.[10]

It's hard for me to imagine how any girl or young woman would not think twice about having sex outside of marriage once they are informed of the bonding aspect that has been proven with oxyto-cin. I can't help but wonder if perhaps it would have impacted my decision as a teen girl. Of course, for a girl who thinks she is in love, "bonding" sounds like a positive rather than a negative. For me personally, it explains so much of my attachment to my high school boyfriend after we became sexually active. Jealousy, insecurity, and an overall possessiveness entered our relationship. Once physical intimacies have been exchanged, pulling back from the relation-ship is difficult and recovering when a breakup occurs is even more difficult than for those who did not swap physical intimacies. If your daughter is a teen, chances are, she has witnessed this pattern in play, whether she has experienced it firsthand or witnessed it among her friends who "bond" through sex or sexual activity and then struggle to "detach" emotionally in the aftermath. As much as our girls have been brainwashed by the culture to believe sex is "no big deal," reality will teach them otherwise. As Paul advised, "The body, however, is not meant for sexual immorality but for the Lord, and the Lord for the body" (1 Cor. 6:13).

Early Sex and Mental Health

Numerous studies have noted an increase in depression among sexually active girls. The National Longitudinal Survey of Adolescent Health found that 25.3 percent of sexually active girls ages fourteen to seventeen reported that they felt depressed "a lot of the time" or "most all of the time," as compared with 7.7 percent who were not sexually active.[11] Another study of sixty-five hundred adolescents found that sexually active teenage girls were more than three times as likely to be depressed and nearly three times as likely to have had a suicide attempt than girls who were not sexually active.[12]

If you ever doubted that girls have a harder time separating their emotions from the physical act of sex, another study published in the *Journal of Health and Social Behavior* analyzed the data on eight thousand teens and found that "females experience a larger increase in depression than males in response to romantic involvement," and that "females' greater vulnerability to romantic involvement may explain the higher rates of depression in female teens."[13]

Obviously the evidence continues to mount, yet stop and think about it. How often do you recall the media exposing the results of these reputable studies? It amazes me that you can find warning labels on just about everything imaginable, yet when it comes to warning our young women about side effects linked to out-of-wedlock sex, such as depression (among many others), mum's the word. Even the medical community is encouraged to remain silent lest they infringe upon a young woman's personal choice. No doubt they would speak up should a young patient admit to smoking. They would likely launch into a lecture regarding the dangers associated with smoking and the increased risk for lung cancer and emphysema. Yet culture's only concern seems to be with protection from STDs and unplanned pregnancies. Unfortunately, condoms and birth control pills can't protect the psyche.

STDs: The Real Truth

STDs are diseases that are passed from one person to another through sexual contact. Some STDs include chlamydia, gonorrhea, genital herpes, human papillomavirus (HPV), syphilis, and HIV. American teens and young adults ages fifteen to twenty-four make up 27 percent of the sexually active population yet account for 50 percent of the twenty million new STIs in the U.S. each year.[14]

Many have no idea they are infected because many STI's often have no immediate symptoms and may not become apparent for years.[15] Additionally, young women's bodies are biologically more prone to STDs.[16]

HPV is the most common sexually transmitted infection (STI). Approximately, seventy-nine million Americans, most in their late teens and early twenties, are infected with HPV. According to the Centers for Disease Control, there are many different types of HPV and some types can cause health problems including genital warts and cancers. You can get HPV by having vaginal, anal, or oral sex with someone who has the virus. It is most commonly spread during vaginal or anal sex. HPV can be passed even when an infected person has no signs or symptoms.[17]

And then there's chlamydia. According to the Centers for Disease Control, chlamydia remains the most commonly reported infectious disease in the United States. If untreated, it can spread to the uterus and fallopian tubes (tubes that carry fertilized eggs from the ovaries to the uterus). This can cause pelvic inflammatory disease (PID). Even if it doesn't cause symptoms initially, PID can cause permanent damage to your reproductive system. PID can lead to long-term pelvic pain, inability to get pregnant, and potentially deadly ectopic pregnancy (pregnancy outside the uterus). Chlamydia is easily cured, but can make it difficult to get pregnant if left untreated.[18]

An anonymous physician at a large university health center, penned the book *Unprotected: A Campus Psychiatrist Reveals How Political Correctness in Her Profession Endangers Every Student*, has been sounding the alarm for some time about chlamydia:

> We do know that most women who have been infected
> discover it in a startling way—when they can't conceive.

Since in up to eighty percent of infected women, Chlamydia produces no pain, fever, or discharge, a woman thinks she's fine. Like her infected cells, she's an unsuspecting hostess to a dangerous guest. Years later, when she's settled down, married, and put the partying and hookups behind her; she's told that her blood has antichlamydial antibodies—evidence of an old infection. The doctor puts a scope through her navel to look at her fallopian tubes, and discovers they are enlarged and scarred by adhesions. And this is the reason she cannot have a baby.[19]

She further notes that risk factors that lead to chlamydia are intercourse at an early age, many partners, and possibly even the use of oral contraceptives.[20]

In addition, the author makes the following observation that should serve as a wake-up call to every mother reading this that we are on our own when it comes to informing our daughters of the dangers that can come from STDs. She brilliantly compares how the Journal of American College Health sees the issue of osteoporosis prevention to that of infertility that can result from STDs. Here is what the journal says in regard to osteoporosis:

College students of all ages deserve to be educated about the risk factors that lead to osteoporosis. Young women, in particular, need to be informed about how proper nutrition and regular exercise can help them achieve optimal peak bone mass. They need to be aware that a diet low in calcium and vitamin D as well as smoking, alcohol abuse, steroid use, high-protein diets, and both physical inactivity and excessive exercise may have a negative impact on the lifetime health of their bone structure and may predispose them to a higher risk of osteoporosis in later years.[21]

What does this same journal have to say about infertility that can result from STDs? Nothing. Nada. Not even a peep. Our anonymous campus physician asks this question: "If there is a need to educate a twenty-something-year-old woman about the prevention of a postmenopausal condition, is there not an equal or greater need to make sure she's well-informed about fertility? Given that many college women postpone childbearing longer than ever, and others expose themselves to genital bacteria and viruses, one might wonder why we don't find a warning of this sort in the campus health literature."[22] This sort of political correctness run amok is enough to make your blood boil. This brave M.D. confessed to writing this book after being hushed time and time again in attempts to share the risks associated with sex with the students visiting her clinic. Mothers, clearly the burden is on us to pass along this vital information to our daughters so they can make a truly informed decision.

Teen Pregnancy

Almost 1,700 teenage girls get pregnant every single day. That's seventy girls every hour.[23] Roughly 82 percent of teenage pregnancies aren't planned.[24] Even though teen pregnancy rates have been on the decline and are at an all-time low, three in ten American teen girls still experience pregnancy.[25] Evidence suggests the recent declines are likely due to more teens abstaining from sexual activity, and more teens who are sexually active using birth control than in previous years.[26] This is certainly good news. Unfortunately, even with the decrease, we still have a long way to go when it comes to educating our daughters about the risks associated with teen pregnancy.

Consider that:

* Only 38 percent of teen mothers who have a child before they turn eighteen have a high school diploma, and less than 2 percent earn a college degree by age thirty.[27]
* Thirty percent of teenage girls who drop out of high school do so because of pregnancy or parenthood.[28]
* Two-thirds of young unmarried mothers are poor, with 25 percent going on welfare within three years of a child's birth.[29]
* Compared to the teenage birth rates in other developed countries, America's are the highest: twice as high as Australia's and Canada's, three times as high as France's, three and a half times as high as Germany's, six times as high as the Netherlands', and seven times as high as Japan's.[30]
* Only 20 percent of fathers of children born to teen moms marry the mothers.[31]

Teen pregnancy can literally change the trajectory of our daughters' lives. And yet, the National Campaign to Prevent Teen Pregnancy found that 94 percent of teens want a strong message from society not to have sex, at least until they are out of high school.[32] It will be up to us to bring that message. They certainly won't hear it from the culture or media influences.

Abortion: Anything but a Quick Fix

She was barely seventeen when she went in for her "procedure." No one knew she was pregnant except her boyfriend and a coworker who had recommended the clinic. She was pro-choice, so it was a no-brainer decision. She was a junior and on the varsity cheerleading squad with plans to attend college after graduation. Her boyfriend seemed to struggle more with the decision, as it was hard to reconcile with his Catholic upbringing. However, he agreed that there was no other viable alternative. He was a graduating senior and had been awarded a soccer scholarship at a prestigious university. They called the clinic and felt relieved when a date was on the calendar.

On the morning of the appointment, her coworker called the high school and pretended to be her mother and informed them that she was ill and would not be in school that day. Her boyfriend normally drove her to school in the mornings, so her parents didn't suspect a thing when he pulled into the driveway on that morning in November. Little was said during the twenty-mile drive to the clinic on the outskirts of town. He seemed to be focused on the directions to ensure that they didn't get lost. She fumbled with the radio, looking for anything to distract her from thinking about the procedure. She couldn't even bring herself to say the word in her mind.

Finally they arrived. As they entered the waiting room, she noticed several other girls that appeared to be close to her age, some alone, and a few with their boyfriends. Another girl, who was clearly much younger, sat stoically next to her mother. She wondered for a moment about their stories. She checked in at the window and was immediately handed a mound of paperwork. Her boyfriend settled the bill, paying $250 in cash. After filling out the paperwork, she and her boyfriend passed the time by playing hangman and tic-tac-toe on a scratch sheet of paper. The wait in the waiting room seemed like forever, when in actuality it was less than a half-hour.

She was startled when she heard her name called by a nurse standing in the doorway of the waiting room. She stood and briefly looked back at her boyfriend. He gave her a gentle nod of reassurance as she walked toward the nurse. She didn't look back again as she walked through the doorway and was ushered down a narrow corridor. After a blood test and a brief meeting with a nurse to confirm her decision to move forward with the procedure, she was led into a cold and sterile room.

The details after that were a blur, gray and devoid of detail. A brief introduction by a doctor in a white lab coat. A friendly nurse who held her hand as the anesthesia was administered. Then nothing. Her next memory was waking up in a larger room with many beds, each closed off by curtains. She was alone for a few minutes until a nurse came to her side and informed her that she was in recovery.

The nurse asked her if she had brought anyone with her and if so, would she like for her friend to join her in the recovery room? She nodded her head and softly gave her boyfriend's name. She was not in any pain, but her mind was racing. She began to cry softly. She didn't want to call attention to herself, so she tried to muffle her sobs by turning her head into her pillow. She had thought she would have felt nothing but sheer relief, so the tears caught her off guard. When she looked up, her boyfriend was at her side. He seemed uncertain as to how to respond to her sadness. He fidgeted nervously and leaned down and whispered, "We'll be out of here soon."

By the end of the week, she was cheering at the football game and back into her normal routine. She and her boyfriend would continue to date for another couple of years. From time to time, she would be caught off guard by a sudden remembrance and the tears would flow in secret. This would continue for many years.

I am all too familiar with the pain that can surface unexpectedly, years after an abortion. The story above is my story. The guilt and shame continued to plague me that following year. It was as if a button had been pushed, and suddenly a floodgate of pent-up emotions had come to the surface. In the summer after my junior year of college, a friend would invite me to a Christian retreat for college students being held over the Labor Day weekend. I responded to the gospel of Jesus Christ after hearing about the offer of God's forgiveness. The abortion was forefront in my mind that evening when I bowed my head and prayed. I welcomed this forgiveness and a new life that was being offered.

It would take another decade (and a bit of counseling) for me finally to accept that God had forgiven me for the abortion. By that time, I had married and had three children. Each pregnancy and birth experience served as further confirmation that abortion is anything but a quick fix and every child is, in fact, a gift from God. Today God has done a mighty work in my life, and I am no longer in bondage to the shame.

Surveys indicate that approximately one in three women reading this right now has experienced an abortion. The Alan Guttmacher Institute has determined that by age forty-five, one out of every 2.5 women in the U.S. has had at least one abortion.[33] Roughly 18 percent of women having abortions in the U.S. are teens.[34] Women in their twenties accounted for the majority (58.9%) of abortions in 2014.[35] I am discouraged that over three decades have passed since my abortion and women today are still not being told the whole truth when it comes to abortion. It continues to be peddled as a "quick fix" solution to enable a woman to move on with her life. Yet the truth is, most women are unable to have the procedure and put it out of their minds from that point forward. In fact, the Guttmacher study above found that with the passing of time, negative emotions like sadness and regret increased, and decision satisfaction decreased. That is, more women reported sadness and regret two years following an abortion than one month after the event.[36]

Given that most abortions are among women in their twenties, we must make sure our daughters know the truth before they leave home. If you are reading this and have experienced one or more abortions and you still carry guilt and shame, I implore you to share your story with a strong and supportive Christian friend or mentor. It may even be necessary to see a Christian counselor, as I did years ago. You have been forgiven and God never intended you to carry a load of shame. Romans 8:1 reminds us, "There is therefore now no condemnation for those who are in Christ Jesus" (ESV). There is no sin too big for God's forgiveness and mercy. It is my prayer that you know that and are walking in freedom.

The Verdict Is In

When you tally up all the life-altering possibilities related to sex outside of God's design, it points to the common-sense wisdom that sex was designed for marriage. Whether it's fallout related to hooking up, STDs, unplanned pregnancy, abortion and other outcomes that literally can change the trajectory of a life, the reality is that they can all be prevented by holding to God's design; that sex should be saved for marriage. By committing to that position, as difficult as it may be, our daughters can avoid the heartache that comes with any of the above fallout. God's design for sex is a design that simply, makes sense. Rather than use the above information as a means to pepper our daughters with scare tactics related to the fallout that can occur from sex outside of marriage, I want to encourage you to present the information with the higher goal of working upon her reason. Help her to see that when we engage in sex outside of God's design and plan, we by default, expose ourselves to risks and long-term consequences that He never intended. They need to understand that God's design for sex in marriage is to protect us. It is rooted in His love for us and a desire that we experience life in all its fullness. That life can be found by walking with Him and abiding by His Truths. It is there that our happiness is found. A happiness that far exceeds any momentary thrill that might be gained from hooking up or engaging in sex outside of His intended design.

In order to break down the material in a way that is easier to discuss with your daughter, I have provided some fact sheets related to the risks associated with sex outside of marriage in the appendix. I would recommend that you sit down with your daughter before she enters high school and go over each of the three fact sheets separately. Take her out for dinner or dessert or if it's easier to cover it all at once, consider taking a weekend getaway where you can mix some fun into your conversations. It would be beneficial to go over the talk sheets yearly until she leaves the nest, especially since she will continue to be bombarded with the message that sex outside of marriage is no big deal. The evidence is clear that nothing could be further from the truth. If you don't tell your daughter, who will?

Chapter 9

A New and Improved
Sex Talk

● ● ● ● ● ●

"And you must commit yourselves wholeheartedly to these
commands that I am giving you today. Repeat them again
and again to your children. Talk about them when you are
at home and when you are on the road, when you are going
to bed and when you are getting up." (Deut. 6:6–7 NLT)

I will never forget the night I was tucking Paige into bed and she asked for the first time, "Mom, where do babies come from?" She was ten years old and in the fifth grade. Old enough, I thought, to handle the truth. I told her that "sex is a beautiful act to be enjoyed by a husband and wife in marriage" and then proceeded to launch into the mechanics of sex. Before I ever had a chance to finish, she held her hand in the air and yelled, "Stop! That is the absolute grossest thing I have ever heard. Please tell me you and Daddy have never done that!"

Maybe you have a similar story. The sex talk has never been easy or comfortable, but it is necessary if we are to raise healthy, well-adjusted children. Where do we begin? What do we say? How much do we share? Most Christian parents feel like they're ahead of the curve if they can manage to deliver the standard sex talk to their child at least once before they walk across the stage at graduation. And often that talk boils down to a basic message of "don't do it until you're married because God says to wait." Because it is limited in scope, it fails to recognize that other necessary conversations need to be covered if we are to give our children a more comprehensive view of sex education. This chapter will detail other critical conversations to consider having with your daughter.

The Best Sex-Ed Teacher Your Daughter Will Have Is YOU

When talking to our daughters about sexual purity, we could easily give up and declare defeat. Trust me, plenty of parents have. I am always amazed by the focus many parents place on academics and/or extracurricular activities and the lack of concern over integrity, virtue, and moral character. Mom and Dad will take off work to shuttle their daughters all over town (and out of town) for school or club sports, but when it comes to setting their alarms for church, forget it. That's the only day to sleep in, for heaven's sake! (Or so we're told.) And from what I can tell, the problem is just as bad among Christians. Parents are pooped out from pouring their energy into things that won't matter for eternity and left with little time to disciple their kids. It's no surprise that most Christian kids are behaving just like the rest of the world. Most of us are claiming Proverbs 22:6, "Train a child in the way he should go, and when he is old he will not turn from it," but the truth is, little training is going on.

When teaching our daughters "the way she should go" regarding sex, many moms feel like it's a lost cause given the climate of the culture and the high number of kids (including Christian kids) who give in. You're not likely to fall in that category, or you wouldn't have picked up this book. However, I'm sure we can all think of parents who are standing on the sidelines and scratching their heads, oblivious to what's shaking down around them. And then there are the parents who make excuses, discounting the problem with ridiculous clichés like, "Kids will be kids," and "You're only young once."

Study after study confirms that there is a direct link between engaged, caring parents and children making wise choices. Don't ever doubt the power you have in influencing your daughter when it comes to sexual purity. One study indicated that teenagers in grades eight through eleven who perceive that their mother disapproves of them engaging in sexual intercourse are more likely than their peers to delay sexual activity.[1]

The National Campaign to Prevent Teen Pregnancy conducted a survey that questioned one thousand young people ages twelve to nineteen and 1,008 adults age twenty and older and found that 45 percent of teens said their parents most influence their decisions about sex compared to 31 percent who said their friends are most influential. Religious leaders were only the most influential among 7 percent, while teachers and sex educators stood at 6 percent and the media at 4 percent.[2] Given this information, let's take a look at four key factors that, if in place, can help reinforce God's design for sex and therefore, a commitment to sexual purity.

1. Open Lines of Communication

A key factor in raising daughters who desire sexual purity is to talk about it. A good rule of thumb to remember when it comes to discussing sex is to keep the conversation simple and keep it going. The first step is making sure your daughter has a grasp of what the purpose of sex is and what God has to say about it. It doesn't have to be complicated, and, in fact, it needs to be simple enough for a youngster to grasp, as many will begin asking questions about sex in grade school. I love the approach that sexual abstinence expert Pam Stenzel takes in her book *Sex Has a Price Tag: Discussions about Sexuality, Spirituality, and Self-Respect.* Here it is in a nutshell:

1. Humans did not create sex, God did.
2. Since God created sex, He's the one who understands it the best.
3. Since God understands sex better than anyone, a person who wants to have great sex (and why would anyone want to have rotten sex?) needs to know what God says about sex.

What does God have to say about sex? Sex was created for one, and only one, situation—marriage.[3]

Once they are clear on the basics regarding the purpose of sex and God's view of sex, then you can begin to incorporate some of the information we have discussed into your conversations, assuming, of course, your daughter is old enough. Break down the information into bite-size conversations rather than dumping an entire chapter's worth of information on her at one time. Build stories around the statistics we have addressed in order to bring them to life.

Your daughter should have a good grasp on what the culture is not telling her about sex (chapter 8) before she enters high school.

(Note: Depending on her level of understanding and maturity, she may need to hear this information in middle school.) Continue the conversations over the years, taking advantage of teachable moments as they occur. For example, if you see a sexually suggestive storyline or scene on TV or in a movie, talk about it. Most of the shows popular among teens assume sex is a normal part of life for teens.

When talking to your daughter, provide opportunities for two-way communication. One survey found that 88 percent of teens said it would be easier to postpone sexual activity and avoid teen pregnancy if they were able to have more open, honest conversations about sex with their parents. Interestingly, the same study found that only 32 percent of adults surveyed believe parents are most influential in their teens' decisions about sex.[4]

2. Relationship

One study found that teenagers who "feel highly connected to their parents and report that their parents are warm, caring and supportive—are far more likely to delay sexual activity than their peers."[5] Another unrelated study found that close relationships with mothers seemed to discourage youngsters from sexual activity. However, I should note that it also found that the effect diminished with age and, among girls, disappeared altogether. Author of the study, Barbara Huberman, notes, "High levels of mother-teen connectedness were not significantly associated with delays in sexual intercourse among 10th-11th-grade girls." She offered the explanation that "girls in their late teens generally felt a powerful need to claim their independence, in part by defying their mothers."[6]

All the more reason, moms, to establish the relationship early on and begin the conversations when the time is right. If (or when) the relationship becomes tenuous, we can rest in the knowledge that we have provided them with the facts along the way. And while I concur with Ms. Huberman's assessment that "girls in their late teens generally felt a powerful need to claim their independence," I'm not so sure I agree with her conclusion that many girls will do it for the sheer sake of "defying their mothers." The relationship doesn't have to be fractured during these years, just different. It's important that we don't allow our daughters to push us away in these years and that we fight to keep the lines of communication open.

3. *Boundaries/Supervision*

When talking to our daughters about sex, Sarah Brown, director of the National Campaign to Prevent Teen Pregnancy, said that talk alone is insufficient. She further stated that what matters even more, especially among younger teenagers, is a relationship in which parents keep close tabs on them, knowing who their friends are and what they do together. Amazing. Imagine that—deep down inside, our children feel more loved and cared for when they have boundaries and supervision. They want their parents to be parents, not their buddies. Brown concluded that the ideal home for fostering this kind of closeness is one open to friends of the children. She said, "When a house is open to young people, there is this sense they can be themselves. There's food, space, caring adults around."[7]

When my oldest son entered high school, we added a game room onto the back of our house and declared, "This is the hangout. Your friends are welcome here." You don't have to take out a loan and build a game room. All you need is one spare room and an open heart. I have heard of others converting garages into an extra space or using an extra living room. Be creative. The important thing is to establish some safe spaces for your children to hang out with adult supervision.

4. Faith

As we enter into the age of a post-Christian nation, Christians who truly look to the Bible to guide them in making moral decisions will become an embattled minority. Consider that in a Barna survey that asked teens if they agreed that sex before marriage is morally wrong, only 5 percent of teens that fell into the category of "no faith" agreed. Among teens that fell into the category of "unchurched Christian," only 14 percent agreed. Sadly, among teens that fell into the category of "churched Christian," only 25 percent agreed. However, one category stood out from the pack. Among the Christians who fell into the category of "engaged Christian," 76 percent believed that sex before marriage is morally wrong.[8] How engaged your child is in the faith will have a huge impact on their view of sex. Clearly, it is not enough to take our children to church and assume they will walk away with moral convictions based on biblical principles and standards. An "engaged Christian" is just that—engaged. They read their Bibles, pray consistently, and most likely have parents who view church as supplementary to the teaching they are receiving at home. If your family is not engaged in the faith, take some time to search your heart and discover why that is. Our assigned purpose in life is to "know God and make Him known." When Christ is at the center of our lives and we model that to our children, we send a clear message that this life was never intended to be about us. An engaged Christian follows after God rather than the pleasures of this world.

An Added Conversation about Sexting

A few years ago, a mom friend of mine shared with me a harrowing tale that involved her ninth-grade daughter texting her boyfriend a topless picture at his request. Before I go any further, let me vouch for her daughter in saying she is a sweet Christian girl who is actively involved in her youth group at her local church and Bible study. Additionally, her mom is the kind of mom who engages in conversations and takes an active role in discipling her and her siblings (as does her father). I share this to make the point that any one of us could have been in this mother's shoes and any one of our daughters could have been tempted to do what her daughter did. Girls today are under immense amounts of pressure to engage in sexting as the culture has normalized it as a standard rite of passage. So, back to my story. As you probably imagined, it didn't end well. Upon breaking up, the boy sent the picture to his friends, and her daughter suffered so much embarrassment and shame, she ended up in counseling and withdrew from school to be home-schooled for the remainder of the year. She eventually returned to school but her emotional scars remain.

Studies suggest that sexting is more common than many parents might realize or want to admit. Sexting is defined as the sending or receiving of nude or seminude images or sexually explicit text messages. More than half the undergraduate students who took part in an anonymous online survey said they sexted when they were teenagers. Nearly 30 percent said they included photos in their sexts, and 61 percent were unaware that sending nude photos via text could be considered child pornography.[9] The survey also found that only 2 percent of respondents reported that they notified a parent or teacher about a sext that they received.[10] For teenagers, this scenario often happens in a dating situation or one where they like each other and one teenager (usually the female) is asked to "prove" they like the other person. That is the scenario my friend's daughter found herself in.

Sexting can also happen when one person sends a nude or semi-nude photo to another without asking for consent first. I recently had an 8th grade girl tell me that it is common for girls in her grade to receive "d*ck pics" from the boys (of themselves in an aroused state). When I asked why a boy would do that, she said it was to bait which girls might respond and in turn, agree to send nude pictures back. Noting my shock, she laughed it off and casually responded, "It's just what boys do." Boys who, no doubt, have logged many hours viewing porn and as a result, have normalized a depraved behavior to the degree that it would never occur to them that the girls in their grade were worthy of respect and honor. She went on to say that she and her friends think it's stupid and just delete them when they get them, but some girls think it's funny and like the attention.

With all the recent progress that has been made in bringing sexual harassment and abuse into the spotlight and empowering women to come forward and speak up, how is it that our youngest generation of girls has slipped through the cracks? Where did they get the idea that receiving nude pictures from their male classmates is perfectly normal behavior and something they must willingly tolerate? How in the world did we get here? Let me take a stab at answering that question. When you have a generation of boys, most of which have been brought up in the schoolroom of the culture, who have relentlessly been lured by the porn industry to become loyal, dependent, and life-long consumers who have in their possession a device that allows them to access that electronic drug on demand, free of charge, and with total anonymity, the fall-out will be immense. Couple that with the fact that there is little shame associated with viewing porn among those in this emerging generation and that most porn centers on the theme that women are nothing more than objects who exist to satisfy the sexual urges of men. Now, add to that equation a generation of young women, most of which have been brought up in the schoolroom of the culture and bombarded with message after message through media, advertising, and the entertainment industry, that their sole purpose is to cultivate their sexuality and sensuality (long before they even know what that is, mind you) in an effort to capture the attention of the opposite sex. Add to that the lack of frontal lobe development in adolescents that often leads them to engage in high-risk behaviors with little thought of consequences. Consequences mind you that in this case could include criminal charges, tattered reputations, addictions, and for some young women, shame so immense they consider taking their lives. Sexting is a huge deal. Porn is a huge deal. We must be intentional when it comes to talking to our daughters (and sons) about the consequences of both. As mothers, we need to educate our daughters that they are worthy of dignity and respect. Even if you feel confident your daughter would not consent to sexting or sending a nude image, chances are, she could find herself on the receiving end of an uninvited sext (nude image or talk) or a request for a picture given the prevalence of the behavior.

Talk to your daughter about sexting and make sure she knows it is a form of sexual harassment or even, sexual abuse to receive uninvited sexually explicit texts or images. It has taken adult women long enough to gain the courage to speak up against inappropriate and offensive sexual banter, and we must raise our daughters to know it's okay to speak up, as well. "Boys will only be boys" if we allow them to do as they please with no consequences for their actions. In the Appendix, I have provided a talk sheet on sexting, sexual assault, and sexual violence to assist you in your conversations with your daughter.

An Added Conversation about Porn

Our children are growing up in a culture that views porn as harmless fun. According to a Barna survey of teens and young adults (ages thirteen to twenty-four), only 32 percent say "viewing porn is wrong."[11] "The vast majority reports that conversations with their friends about porn are neutral, accepting or even encouraging. Just one in ten teens and one in twenty young adults report talking with their friends about porn in a disapproving way."[12] The Barna survey also found that when teens and young adults in the survey were asked to rank a series of actions (lying, stealing, etc.) on a five-point scale based on "always okay," "usually okay," "neither wrong nor okay," "usually wrong, " and "always wrong," teens and young adults ranked "not recycling" as more immoral than viewing pornographic images. "Not recycling" ranked #4, "significant consumption of electricity or water" ranked #7, and "viewing pornographic images" was all the way down at #9.[13] Porn is anything but harmless.

Researchers at the University of New Hampshire found that about 90 percent of children between the ages of eight and sixteen have looked at porn. In fact, the largest group of Internet pornography consumers are between the ages of twelve and seventeen. The study also found that most kids who watch porn on the computer weren't searching for it the first time they found it.[14] While porn is more prevalent among young men, it is on the rise among our young women. A Barna survey that researched attitudes and use of porn in the digital age found that "twice as many male teens and young adults use porn than female teens and young adults (67 percent compared to 33 percent). In other words, 33 percent of girls and women ages thirteen to twenty-four reported being frequent porn users. Perhaps even more disturbing is the moral ambiguity to porn by teens and young adults (ages thirteen to twenty-four).[15]

Mary Anne Layden, co-director of the Sexual Trauma and Psychopathology Program at the University of Pennsylvania's Center for Cognitive Therapy, called porn the "most concerning thing to psychological health that I know of existing today." She further notes, "The internet is a perfect drug delivery system because you are anonymous, aroused, and have role models for these behaviors," Layden said. "To have drugs pumped into your house 24/7, free, and children know how to use it better than grown-ups know how to use it—it's a perfect delivery system if we want to have a whole generation of young addicts who will never have the drug out of their mind. . . . Pornography addicts have a more difficult time recovering from their addiction than cocaine addicts since coke users can get the drug out of their system, but pornographic images stay in the brain forever."[16]

It's easy to feel like the situation is hopeless when hearing these disturbing findings. While porn is a sad reality of our times, it doesn't diminish the power of God. As mothers we will simply need to step up our game and come up with a new and improved battle plan. Our battle plan must go beyond activating parental controls and telling our children not to look when they see it. That will not be enough. We need to take it a step further and teach our children to monitor their hearts. Just as Proverbs 4:23 reminds us, "Above all else, guard your heart, for it is the wellspring of life." Our children are not likely to embrace the importance of monitoring and guarding their hearts in the moment unless they understand that viewing porn leads to a diminished quality of life.

Believe it or not, the Bible talks about pornography. In the New Testament there are twenty-six references to *porneia* (the Greek word in which our English word *porn* is derived. Porneia is translated as "fornication," "whoredom" or "sexual immorality." When spoken of in the Bible we are told that our bodies are not made for porneia (1 Cor. 6:13); we should run from it (1 Cor. 6:18); we should not seek it out (1 Cor. 7:2); and we should repent if we fall prey to it (2 Cor. 12:21). The antidote to indulging in the temptation of porneia is a life of purity, which can only be obtained by the process of sanctification or being made holy with the help of the Holy Spirit living within us. In other words, our children will need the power of God to stand against this temptation and are not likely to conquer it in their own mortal strength. Because God wired or bodies for intimacy and relationship with Him first and foremost, nothing else will fill that need. Porn is a false substitute that promises intimacy in the moment, but in truth, robs the user by leaving them disabled when it comes to true intimacy in their real-life relationships. Most importantly, it robs them of spiritual intimacy with God.

Part of educating our children about the damage and fallout of viewing porn is making sure they understand it is a tool of the enemy to "steal, kill, and destroy" and thus, rob them of the abundant life God intended them to have (John 10:10). The world will certainly not be teaching them this truth and it's up to us to make sure they understand that by buying into the lie that viewing porn is harmless, they have essentially been conned by the enemy. For many of our children, knowledge of this truth may not be enough to ward off the temptation, but I can assure you once they have fallen into the enemy's trap, they will be aware of the emptiness that results. It should come as no surprise that existing studies have found the "frequency of porn viewing correlates with depression, anxiety, stress and social malfunction, as well as less sexual and relationship satisfaction and altered sexual tastes, poorer quality of life and health, and real-life intimacy problems."[17] Author William Struthers, in his book *Wired for Intimacy* says, "Pornography is a sin that robs God of his glory in the gift of sex and sexuality. We have long known that sin takes hostages."[18] As mothers, we must make sure our children know that porn is a big deal and can impact their future marriages, as well as their future happiness. We must not naively believe that porn is only a temptation for boys and men. As mothers, we must address this topic and speak to this emptiness that results from viewing porn. More importantly, we must offer our children the hope that it's never too late to turn back to God for help and take Him up on His offer of the "abundant life."

We need to diligently teach our daughters that God wired our bodies for intimacy and relationship with Him first and foremost; nothing else will fill that need. Porn is a false substitute that promises intimacy in the moment, but in truth, robs the user by leaving them disabled when it comes to true intimacy in their real-life relationships. Most importantly, it robs them of spiritual intimacy with God.

If You Suspect Your Daughter Is Having Sex

Maybe as you are reading this, you suspect that your daughter has already had sex and you're left wondering where to go from here. Certainly, you don't give up that battle and declare defeat. The evidence presented reminds us that there is great benefit to committing to secondary virginity as well as support for the number of sexual partners influencing the future of marriage and happiness. It could be that your daughter is having sex, but she desires to change. (Remember, statistics show that nearly two-thirds of girls regret their decision to have sex and wish they had waited.) In this situation I would highly recommend that you meet with her on a weekly basis to discuss the talk sheets provided for this conversation in the Appendix. (Ideally, these should be discussed before she engages in sexual activity, but better late than never.) Draw boundaries and supervise your daughter. Be picky about who she dates (if she's allowed to date) and let her know that the lines of communication are open. Most importantly, remind her that she is forgiven of her sin and that God's best for her from this point forward is a renewed commitment to sexual purity. There is no need to beat her over the head with her sin and shame her. That's not God's way, and it shouldn't be our way either. Romans 8:1 reminds us, "There is no condemnation for those who belong to Christ Jesus" (NLT).

On the other hand, if after discussing the matter with your daughter, you discover that she is unrepentant, it is most likely because (1) she doesn't want to risk losing her boyfriend or (2) she has wandered from the path of God and is callous to His truth regarding sex outside of marriage. Regardless, you must open up the lines of communication in an effort to begin conversations about the information we have discussed. When talking to her, emphasize that your motive is concern, love, and her future well-being. This is a tricky dance, especially if you've come to the conclusion that she should no longer see this young man while she lives under your roof. If that is a boundary you need to draw, I encourage you to draw it while, at the same time, reminding her that your motive is love. Yes, there is always the risk that she will enter into an all-out rebellion and continue down her wayward path. The sobering truth is that, if she wants to find a way to continue having sex with her boyfriend (or hooking up), she will find a way, even while living under your roof. I would begin by praying for the right time and setting to approach your daughter. Ask God to do a mighty work on her heart in advance. Prayer will be your most powerful force. You cannot sway her heart, but God can.

How Much Should You Share about Your Past?

This is perhaps the most common question I receive from mothers when I speak at parenting conferences. Most of us, truth be told, made plenty of mistakes along the way and wrestle with how much information, if any, we should share with our daughters. Here are some general rules when it comes to sharing:

* Never share details with your daughter related to the number of guys you may have slept with or specific details about what you did. Doing so does not serve a purpose and falls under the category of TMI (too much information). For example, I shared with my daughter, "I was not a virgin when I married, and I regret my decision not to wait." The focus should be the regret rather than the act itself.

* Never share information regarding your past with your daughter if she is younger than middle school. Depending on the maturity and temperament of your daughter, she may not be ready for it in middle school. If she is somewhat sheltered and not even displaying an interest in boys, what is the purpose? We want to be preventive, yet at the same time be sensitive not to rob them of their innocence. Whether you are sharing your own regret or the regret of others you knew that gave in, pray and ask God to nudge your heart when the time is right.

* Never share information with your daughter about experiences where you have yet to experience healing. Our daughters are not equipped to help us process guilt

and shame over our past actions. When we share, we must, ourselves, be walking in victory. I am talking about particularly traumatic events we may have experienced as a result of poor choices (extreme promiscuity, the contraction of an STD, an abortion, giving a child up for adoption, alcohol or drug abuse that led to unwanted sex). Such accounts can be valuable to share with our daughters when the time is right; however, we must be at a place in our healing where our motive is to provide our daughters with an example of sincere regret rather than to lean on them for comfort. God has forgiven your sin "as far as the east is from the west" (Ps. 103:12). If you have not embraced that truth, share your pain instead with a trusted Christian friend or counselor who can encourage you in the road to healing.

- Refrain from sharing information related to past sexual abuse with your children. Perhaps they may be ready in their adult years to hear such information, but what is the purpose of telling them this information (unless, of course, they have been abused). A dear friend of mine regrets telling her children this information as they struggled for years with how to process what they had been told. Some issues of our past are better left to a trusted Christian mentor, friend, or perhaps even a Christian counselor.

- Never share information regarding someone else's past in an effort to gain a teachable moment with your daughter unless you have their prior permission. "So-and-so at church shared in our small group Bible study that she got pregnant as a teen and had an abortion." No! "I have a dear friend . . ." would be a better approach but never give names without prior consent. This also goes for girls your daughter's age about whom you may have heard a buzz. Gossip is never justified even if it's intended to be a teachable moment.

Most of us, truth be told, are hesitant to some degree to share our own past regret because we fear that our daughters may walk away with the impression that if "Mom messed up, I can mess up, too." I can't guarantee you that they won't. If your daughter is currently in a rebellious phase and looking for permission to misbehave, she may draw that conclusion. However, if you convey a heartfelt sense of regret mixed with a sincere intent to spare your own daughter from making the same mistakes, I doubt she will race out to repeat your same sin.

Remembering the Real Prize

Many viewpoints exist among Christians regarding the most effective way to address sexual purity. It is oftentimes a heated topic that is fueled by much passion and good intent. No talk comes with a guarantee, but I can say this much: after having these conversations over the years with my own children, I had no regrets. At the end of the day, I told them that the decisions they made regarding sex and sexual activity would be between them and God. My job was to educate them about the risks involved, impress God's Truths upon their hearts, and pray their hearts would be sensitive to His leading, even if it was after the fact. Oftentimes, Christian parents frame the sex talks with our children as a formula to obtain the ultimate prize: virginity until marriage. I am stepping on my own toes, here. There were times when I was guilty of this in my conversations with my children, or for that matter, when talking to young women about sexual purity at past events or in my books. While reaching the goal of wedding night virginity would be ideal, the truth is, God is able to redeem and restore hearts whether that goal is reached or not. How many of us reading this have stories of redeemed and restored hearts after giving up our virginity? We need to stop presenting this topic with the attitude that all is lost if one mistake is made.

The reality is that most of our daughters will not make it to their wedding nights with their virginity intact. If we make that the end-all goal and fail to remind them of God's grace and mercy along the way, they will count themselves as failures and miss what God can do in the aftermath, even if that aftermath comes many years later. I am living proof of that and chances are, you are too. My abortion at the age of seventeen was a huge factor in drawing me to Christ at the age of twenty-one. Today, I share about that experience openly as a reminder that no sin is too big for the forgiveness of Christ. Likewise, my oldest son and my daughter-in-law became pregnant during their engagement. Today, my daughter-in-law leads youth girls in our church and openly shares her story with the girls she mentors. Their unexpected pregnancy with their first child was a turning point in their lives and God used it as a wake-up call to strengthen their faith and remind them how greatly they are loved (and forgiven!). When I think of my story, their story, and the many other redemption stories I've heard from women over the years, I'm reminded that God never, ever gives up on us. He is in the business of bringing beauty from brokenness. I am reminded of that every time I share my story and in doing so, it encourages someone else to receive God's grace and walk away from the shame. I am reminded of God's infinite grace every time I look at my oldest grandson.

The ultimate prize is a restored heart. Whether that heart is restored after sexual sin or some other sin, our daughters need to know that God can make their hearts whole again. He never gives up on them.

Talk about It

· · · · · · · · · ·

Chapter 7

Has the topic of sex come up with your daughter? Did you initiate the conversation or did she?

Did it surprise you to discover that "Evangelical teens don't accept themselves as people who will have sex until they've already had it?" How might this change your approach when it comes to conversations you have with your daughter related to sex?

Have you discussed the benefits of saving sex for marriage with your daughter?

When looking over the Mayo Clinic's age-based suggestions for the recommended topics to discuss related to sex, are you ahead of the game, on target, or behind?

Chapter 8

Have you had a conversation with your daughter about physical fallout from sex such as STDs or teen pregnancy? Are you prepared to educate her as to the long-term effects of many of the common STDs and how they could affect her future? What about an unexpected pregnancy?

How might you introduce the topic of "oxytocin" with your daughter in an effort to reinforce God's purpose for sex in bonding husband and wife? Have you talked to her about the impact of "hooking up," since a bond is created in sex?

Have you discussed with your daughter the emotional fallout that can result from sex outside of marriage?

Have you discussed with your daughter the spiritual fallout that can result from sex outside of marriage? More importantly, have you reminded her that she can always come boldly before the throne of grace?

Chapter 9

After reviewing the four key factors that reinforce God's design for sex, (open communication; relationship; boundaries/supervision; faith), what areas of improvement might you need to make?

Were you aware that surveys show parents are the best sex-ed teachers for their children and have the greatest influence? Do you feel qualified to have conversations related to sex? Why or why not?

Has your daughter been exposed to a sexting situation? Have you discussed the topic of sexting with her? (Assuming she is old enough, of course.)

Have you discussed the topic of porn with your daughter before and specifically, the fallout that can occur from viewing pornography?

When discussing the topic of sex outside of marriage with your daughter, do you emphasize virginity as the ultimate prize or a restored heart?

Conversation 4

Childhood is only for a season.

Chapter 10

Forever Young

● ● ● ● ● ●

When I was a child, I spoke and thought and reasoned
as a child. But when I grew up, I put away childish things.
(1 Cor. 13:11 NLT)

For years, many youth culture experts have expressed concern over the rush for our kids to grow up. While this is true regarding exposure to mature themes due to the availability of information on demand (Internet, smartphones, technology, etc.), it is somewhat of a myth when it comes to the rush to independence and adulthood. Who among us can't recall the excitement of meeting our friends for a movie or to walk around the mall sans our parents? The first taste of freedom that comes with "hanging out" with friends is a benchmark on the road to adulthood. It is in this environment where we learn to sample the real world out from under the protective wing of our parents. We also learn how to navigate interpersonal relationships with our friends, as well as the opposite sex.

For today's youth, hanging out for the most part is a virtual experience. It is a group text or a social media interaction via comments or likes, but rarely does it involve actually going out. *Hanging out* has evolved into *hanging in* with your smartphone or tablet never far from your side. Consider that one in four teens today do not have a driver's license by the time they graduate from high school.[1] The decline in driving appear across all regions, ethnic groups, and socioeconomic classes. When I was a teen, we were begging our parents to get a hardship license so we could drive before the age of sixteen! Getting your driver's license was a major hurdle on the path to adulthood and we were counting down the days to freedom. Many teens today seem to show little urgency to get a license and seem content to have Mom or Dad chauffeur them to school and extracurricular activities for as long as possible.

Add to this the fact that fewer teens seek out summer jobs. In 1980, 70 percent of teens had a summer job as compared to 43 percent in 2010. According to the Bureau of Labor Statistics data, the decrease doesn't seem to be related to a tough job market. The number of teens who want a summer job but can't find one has stayed about the same over the years, but the number of teens who don't want a job has doubled.[2] Many parents argue that due to more stringent college requirements, their teens are unable to work due to the heavy load of homework and extracurricular activities. Author Jean Twenge found this not to be the case. In her book, *iGen*, she analyzed the data and found that "high school seniors heading to college in 2015 spent four fewer hours a week on homework, paid work, volunteer work, and extracurricular activities during their last year in high school than those entering college in 1987."[3] They have more leisure time per day than GenX'ers did. So, what exactly are they doing that takes up so much of their time? Twenge says, look no further than the smartphone they are cradling in the palm of their hands. For many teens, it has filled the gap and become their new, unpaid job. Of course, we know it will come with a price.

The trend of teens not working has also led to the inability of teens to manage money. Allowance for many has become a thing of the past and paid chores are almost unheard of. Teens have come to expect that their expensive toys (electronics, etc.) and leisure activities will be financed on demand by Mom and Dad. When they have a need or want, they simply ask, or (ahem), badger their parents until they wear them down into submission. Why go to the trouble of working extra hours during the week to earn money when all you have to do is hit up the First Bank of Good Ol' Mom and Dad?

What's particularly confusing about this cultural shift in delayed adulthood is that national surveys reveal that an overwhelming majority of Americans, including younger adults, agree that between twenty and twenty-two, people should be finished with school, working and living on their own.[4] Yet in reality many fail to live up to their own expectations for adulthood. Which begs the question: What constitutes an official "adult"? While financial independence (no supplementary income/housing from parents) is an obvious determinant, the pursuit of marriage and parenthood were once viewed as benchmarks for adulthood. Today marriage and parenthood hardly make the radar of this budding generation. Marriage is viewed as something they might start thinking seriously about after they chase their dreams, travel abroad, secure full-time jobs, and find themselves. Good luck with that! Hopefully, by the time they give you grandkids (if they ever do), you're not trying to keep up with them on a walker!

Jean Twenge, author of *iGen*, noted in her study of today's children and teens "the entire developmental trajectory, from childhood to adolescence to adulthood, has slowed." "Adolescence" she claims, "is now an extension of childhood rather than the beginning of adulthood."[5] Her finding is backed up by a recent study of iGen college students (verses students in the 1980s and 1990s). iGen'ers were more likely to agree "I wish that I could return to the security of childhood" and "The happiest time in life is when you are a child." They were less likely to agree "I would rather be an adult than a child" and "I feel happy that I am not a child anymore."[6] What's going on here? If we are to raise our children to be responsible adults, we must be intentional in teaching them that childhood is only for a season.

Adulting Is So Scary!

If you have any doubts that adolescence has been delayed, look no further than the transition to college. To accommodate young adults (not children) who are reluctant to grow up, many college campuses have assumed the role of protective guardian and contributed to the problem of extended adolescence by offering "trigger warnings" to students who might find some lecture material emotionally distressing. I am all for offering a warning to those who have been through truly traumatic events and thus, are emotionally tender regarding subjects or discussions that might trigger a past trauma. However, there is evidence of an increasing use of trigger warnings to warn of content or an opposing viewpoint that might be upsetting to someone. In the book *Good Faith*, authors David Kinnaman and Gabe Lyons argue, "Protecting people from ideas they'd rather not hear is not only laughable but also ultimately harmful to society. Religious liberty and freedom of speech are rights that can only be put to the test at the distressing intersection of differing ideas. If we run away from that crossroads, these freedoms are simply hypothetical."[7] Part of growing up is learning that not everyone will agree with your opinions, values, or ideals. Only in discussing and debating different schools of thought will we learn the tedious balance of introspection and weighing our personal convictions with objectivity. The irony is that today's teens and young adults pride themselves in being more tolerant than previous generations, but it appears their tolerance has limits if it requires them to *tolerate* an opposing viewpoint or position. This is especially true regarding the Christian faith and biblical Truth.

We have already begun to feel the fallout from a culture that now embraces a post-Christian worldview. For example, one Pennsylvania family was ordered by their neighborhood HOA to take down a nativity scene as part of their Christmas lawn decor because a neighbor reported it as personally "offensive." The home-owner, Mark Wivell, refused to remove his nativity and responded, "People get offended by different things, but just because something offends you, doesn't mean the whole world has to change to accommodate you."[8] Wise words to a generation that has been taught otherwise. Maybe the HOA should require the Wivells to post a "trigger warning" sign in their yard in future years as a compromise! We can expect to see more stories like this emerge in the future as this generation of "snowflakes" leaves their emotionally bubble-wrapped environments and discovers to their shock that not everyone shares their same beliefs.

I don't doubt for a minute that there are some that would love to see trigger warnings applied to content in the Bible that fails to support their current worldview. In 1 Corinthians 1:18, Paul warned, "For the word of the cross is folly to those who are perishing, but to us who are being saved it is the power of God" (ESV). Be assured, the gospel will never be silenced this side of heaven, but it is already considered by many to be "offensive." In fact, in 1 Peter 2:8, Jesus is referred to as "a stone of stumbling and a rock of offense" (ESV). As I have mentioned, it has never been more important to model to our children a commitment to "walk in Truth and lead with love."

In doing so, we cannot sacrifice biblical Truth on the altar of love in an attempt to sugarcoat the message. Nor can we sacrifice love for the sake of Truth by focusing on modifying behavior rather than changing hearts. Becoming a follower of Christ requires an introspective look into our rebellion toward a holy God (sin) and own personal depravity (need for forgiveness). Doing so is not pleasant, but it is the cornerstone of the gospel message and the very thing that sets us free. What a travesty should this current generation miss the Good News of the gospel because they have been trained to avoid anything "unpleasant" or "offensive."

Another example of treating young adults like young adolescents is the trend of campuses offering "safe spaces" to help students cope with anxiety before final exams or in the aftermath of upsetting current events. Such was the case in the days following the 2016 presidential election. An article entitled "Coddling Campus Crybabies" posted on FoxNews.com listed some of the universities offering "safe space" therapy:

- Cornell University recently hosted a "cry-in," complete with hot chocolate and tissues for disappointed Hillary Clinton supporters.
- University of Pennsylvania brought in a puppy and a kitten for therapeutic cuddling.
- Tufts University held arts and crafts sessions for students.
- University of Michigan Law School scheduled an event for this Friday called "Post-Election Self-Care with Food and

Play" with "stress-busting self-care activities" including coloring, blowing bubbles, sculpting with Play-Doh and "positive card making."[9]

For heaven's sake, is this nursery school or college?! Ask any veteran who was shipped off to defend their country at this same age what they think about this new trend of "safe spaces" and you're sure to get an earful. If this is our future, we are in a load of trouble should we ever have to depend on this generation in times of hardship or God forbid, a time of war. I doubt older generations are willing to pick up the pieces while a generation of kiddie-adults rushes to their safe spaces to drink hot cocoa, color, and cuddle with puppies and kittens. It's time to put an end to this nonsense and give our children a clear launch plan from childhood to adulthood.

Better Safe Than Sorry?

Recently, I was in a conversation with other adults from my generation (older end of Gen X'ers) and we were laughing about the playgrounds we used to enjoy as children in parks and school yards. Most were constructed of metal and coupled with a hot summer day in Texas with temperatures soaring past 100 degrees, you weren't likely to forget the back of your bare legs cooking on the slide on your way down. Not to mention, many of the slides looked more like a stairway to heaven, so you were careful to hang on tight to the rails on your way up, especially since there was no pea gravel or soft tire shredding to break your fall. If you survived the slide without a fall or 2nd degree burns, you usually made your way to the metal merry-go-round where your friends did their best to see if they could successfully eject you from the centrifugal spinning wheel of death. Bonus points if you threw up due to motion sickness. We grew up in a day and age before socket protectors, baby monitors, car seats, and mandatory seat belt laws. We walked home from school beginning in grade school and many of us were latchkey kids who let ourselves in, prepared our own snacks, did our homework without parental help or supervision (usually with *Gilligan's Island* and *Brady Bunch* on in the background), and somehow, managed to survive and thrive. I'm certainly not suggesting we retreat back to the days absent of common-sense safety measures, but I can't help but wonder if we've gone a bit overboard in protecting our children.

In a recent poll, 70 percent of adults said they thought the world had become less safe for children since they were children. Yet, the evidence suggests they are much safer now.[10] Teens today have fewer car accidents, get fewer tickets, and overall, take fewer risks, in general. And it's not just the parents who are dedicated to the safety of their children—the children are, as well. Teen pregnancy rates are down, teens are less likely to get in a car with someone who's been drinking, and binge drinking has decreased. (Interestingly, they are just as likely to use marijuana as Millennials were because they, like the generation before them, view it is as safer than drinking.) These findings should be a huge encouragement to parents (other than the pot-smoking) and indicate children are listening to their counsel. Yet, parents are still hesitant to loosen the reins in areas where there is minimal risk. Take for example, the age-old pastime of walking home from school. In 1969, 48 percent of elementary and middle school students walked or rode a bicycle to school. By 2009, only 13 percent did so. Among those who lived less than a mile from the school, 35 percent walked or rode their bicycle to school in 2009 as compared to 89 percent in 1969.[11] Many of the things we once enjoyed in our childhood years is now viewed as irresponsible or even dangerous. But why?

In a piece entitled "The Over-Protected Kid," investigative journalist Hanna Rosin argues that "a preoccupation with safety has stripped childhood of independence, risk taking, and discovery—without making it safer."[12] She goes on to suggest that our safety paranoia has resulted in a "continuous and ultimately dramatic decline in children's opportunities to play and explore in their own chosen ways." In the article, she quotes several expert opinions including a Boston College psychologist, Peter Gray who authored an essay called "The Play Deficit." Gray, she says, "chronicles the fallout from the loss of the old childhood culture, and it's a familiar list of the usual ills attributed to Millennials: depression, narcissism, and a decline in empathy. In the past decade, the percentage of college-age kids taking psychiatric medication has spiked, according to a 2012 study by the American College Counseling Association." In fact, a 2011 study from University of Tennessee at Chattanooga found that students with "hovering" or "helicopter" parents were more likely to take medication for anxiety, depression or both."[13] Rosen goes on to say in her article, "Practicing psychologists have written about the unique identity crisis this generation faces—a fear of growing up and, in the words of Brooke Donatone, a New York–based therapist, an inability 'to think for themselves.'"[14]

I believe our tendency to overprotect our children from perceived dangers of the world has clouded our judgment and produced a legion of anxious parents who in turn, have influenced a legion of anxious kids. Is it any surprise that today's children and teens suffer from fear and anxiety at a staggering rate like never seen before? It doesn't help that our newsfeeds are typically filled with links to articles about unknown dangers lurking around every corner. Button batteries, dry drowning, the brain-eating amoeba, laundry detergent pods, and the list goes on. We are exposed to more news than ever before and if we're not careful, we can come to believe these dangers are the norm, rather than the exception. I am stepping on my own toes here and I have had to limit the time I spend on news (including online and through social media) because I realized the greater the exposure, the more it began to heighten my anxiety especially when it related to potential dangers my children or grandchildren could face. I realized the direct correlation in my overly protective tendencies and the uptick in my news intake when I was recently watching some old home movies from when my children were young. I hardly recognized the mother on the videos. In addition to being a much slimmer version of myself, I was shocked to see how incredibly laid-back I was with my children. Whether it was one of my babies pulling up to a precarious and wobbly stand on a piece of furniture with sharp corners or cheering my four-year-old on as he tried the new zipline by himself for the first time from the treehouse to the ground below. I audibly winced out loud at my younger mom self, yet at the same time, marveled at my calm composure. My children had not grown up in a bubble-wrapped environment free from unknown dangers because I was simply unaware. No computers, no smartphones, and no twenty-four-hour news on demand to enlighten me to the doom-and-gloom stories about the dangers my children faced. Truly, ignorance was bliss. Somehow, they managed to survive their childhoods with very few bumps and bruises along the way.

My transition from more of a laid-back parent to an overprotective parent occurred slowly over time, but spiked in my children's older youth years when my news intake increased. In addition, I had begun writing in those years (the early 2000s) on matters of teen culture and was speaking to teen girls across the country. This was the predawn era of social media where tweens and teens were flocking to MySpace.com, internet chat rooms, engaging in instant messaging (IM'ing), and eventually text messaging (though limited at the time due to the high cost of unlimited text messaging). Many of the same parents who had worked overtime to safety-proof their children's play environments and micro-manage their lives were offering little if any supervision when it came to this new and ironically, more dangerous line world. They were, for the most part, clueless. I can't help but wonder if we contributed to the problem by scaring our kids indoors where we could more closely monitor their safety, all the while exposing them to dangers that far out-weighed a fall from a tree or an incident of "stranger-danger." It is my personal belief that parents need to spend less time attempting to manage the dangers our children face in the great outdoors and more time managing the dangers they face on their electronic devices. In other words, we need to decrease screen time and increase outdoor creative play. The best way to do this is to lead by example in our own lives.

Let Yourself Off the Hook

Many moms today have bought into the lie that it is their primary parenting responsibility to make their children's lives as safe and comfortable as possible. They have somehow equated sheltered, overprotective, insulated children to healthier, happy grown adults. The evidence suggests otherwise. Overly cautious children become anxious, vulnerable adults who expect Mom or Dad (or college administrators, employers, etc.) to be there to protect them at every turn from anything that might prove to be unpleasant, put them at risk, or cause them "emotional injury." The truth is, no matter how hard we try, we cannot protect our children from every physical or emotional danger they will encounter. I can't help but wonder if the pressure moms feel to be perfect in their roles as mothers has led to this unhealthy wave of over-parenting. Yet, nowhere in the Bible does it endorse the idea that a mother's responsibility is to ensure her child never feels unsafe or uncomfortable.

Can you imagine if the disciples' mothers had coddled them at every turn? Had they done so, they never would have agreed to follow Jesus, even unto death. The early Christian leaders we read about in the Bible were courageous and took risks for the sake of the gospel. In Matthew 9:37–38, Jesus reminds His disciples, "The harvest is plentiful, but the laborers are few; therefore pray earnestly to the Lord of the harvest to send out laborers into his harvest" (ESV). That call is still relevant for today and yet, I wonder how many of our daughters (and sons) are prepared to answer that call. Jesus didn't issue the call with a minimum age requirement or a liability release to be signed by your parents. In fact, a few chapters later, He gave a more detailed description of the calling in Matthew 16:24– 26. "If anyone would come after me, let him deny himself and take up his cross and follow me. For whoever would save his life will lose it, but whoever loses his life for my sake will find it. For what will it profit a man if he gains the whole world and forfeits his soul?" (ESV). There is nothing "safe" or "comfortable" about that charge. In fact, that charge requires a response from us. Is your response one of trust or fear? The spread of the gospel requires adventure and risk. Jesus offers an interesting parenting paradox: If you want your children to find life in its truest meaning and fullest sense, raise them to be radical and reckless followers of Christ rather than fragile, anxious "adultlescents" who spend decades searching for identity and purpose. On your dime and likely, under your roof. We can parent them now or we may find ourselves stuck with the burdensome task of reparenting them later in the years when we were looking forward to enjoying the fruits of our own hard work.

I believe one of the key reasons the current generation of children and teens is so uncertain about growing up is their declining sense of meaning and purpose. They are like ships without rudders, floating aimlessly and adrift at sea (with life preservers buckled tightly, no doubt!). Consider that among iGen (or Gen Z) youth, just one in five is "enthusiastic about the advent of adulthood."[15] But, here is the good news: the same Barna survey found that 40 percent of engaged Christians are "very excited about becoming an adult," as compared to 16 percent of those with no faith.[16] There is a clear correlation in children raised in engaged Christian homes to a confidence in adulthood and life purpose. Identity and purpose can only be found in our creator, God. Young women who are raised to know that Jesus Christ is their one true north have no desire to remain in the nest under the parent's wing of protection indefinitely. They have a compass to guide them into adulthood. It's up to you to teach them to use that compass.

Chapter 11

Ready, Set, Launch!

● ● ● ● ● ●

*Start children off on the way they should go, and even when
they are old they will not turn from it. (Prov. 22:6)*

It was approximately ten years ago when I dropped my daughter off at college over 800 miles from her childhood home. It wasn't my first rodeo, as I had been down that road before just two years prior with her older brother. Strangely, it wasn't any easier given that I knew what to expect. There was something about dropping off a daughter that was different than dropping off a son, especially given that it was so far from home. Add to the equation that she had never been away from home longer than two weeks in her previous eighteen years. As we said our final goodbyes with hugs and misty eyes, the hardest moment was watching her turn and walk up the walkway to her dorm. She looked so young with her blonde ponytail bouncing behind her. For a split second, I wanted to chase her down and tell her this was a terrible mistake and to come back home and take a gap year. Or five.

As I think back on that moment, I recall being overwhelmed with the "what-ifs." What if she gets sick and I'm not there to take care of her? What if she doesn't find sweet Christian friends? What if she doesn't find a local church to plug into? What if she doesn't bother to look for one in the first place? What if she goes out with guys who try to take advantage of her? What if she settles for a guy who is less than God's best since she hasn't really had a serious dating experience before? At the root of all my "what-ifs" was the fear that her father and I had not adequately prepared her for the launch into adulthood. The irony is that we had, in fact, been intentional in implementing a launch plan with our children to prepare them for this moment, but I was overcome in that moment with the realization that the clock had run out and our time was up. In the back of my mind, I couldn't help but wonder, "Did we fully take advantage of the years God had given us to prepare her for the launch?"

That question would be answered over the next four years. Other than a few minor bumps along the way, she proved she was more than ready to tackle adulthood. She found the most amazing Christian girlfriends, who have become lifelong friends today. She found a wonderful local church and was involved from her freshman year until the time she left. She plugged into a small group Bible study and grew in her faith. She went out with a few duds here and there, but she was quick to recognize they were less than God's best and not worth her time. And she met the most amazing, godly man who I am proud to say is my son-in-law today. But here's the best part: She and her husband (and my sweet granddaughter) live just three miles away and she is one of my very best friends. While my husband I don't take full credit for her transition into adulthood,

we'd like to think our intentionality in having a launch plan to prepare her for adulthood played a factor.

Do you have a launch plan for your daughter? Similar to a real
launch, there are three stages that determine a successful launch: a
prelaunch phase; a test launch phase; and ultimately, a final launch
phase. Even if your daughter is a toddler, it is not too early to think
about a launch plan. Below you will find some ideas for each of the
three critical phases.

Prelaunch: The stage of a girl's life from age two to fourteen
should be viewed as the prelaunch phase. During this stage critical life skills should be introduced, as well as the training required
over the years to help your daughter master life skills. Skills such
as personal responsibility for belongings, money management, goal
setting, time management, and a strong work ethic can be introduced at a young age and cultivated over the years. For example,
my husband did an amazing job in training our children from
a young age with basic money management skills. Beginning in
their preschool years, he taught them to set aside money for tith-
ing, savings, and spending. Each child had three plastic containers
that served as their bank vault. To give them a sense of a strong
work ethic, they were given chores from an early age that matched
their level of ability. Some chores could earn them extra money
while others were performed without pay to teach them the value
of teamwork and doing their part to support the family. He also
taught them at an early age to manage their savings by giving them
each a blank check register book. (I'm sure there's a digital version
of this method today!) When they received allowance or birthday/
Christmas money, they put it in their register to keep track of their
savings. When they spent their money, they deducted the amount.
We recently stumbled upon their old check register books and got

a kick out of seeing their young chicken scratch writing in some of the earlier entries. We got the biggest laugh when we saw deductions by my youngest son for penalties his father gave him such as: "did not brush teeth—50 cents" and "left bike in rain—$1." Most of his savings was drained by penalties and what little was left was spent on candy!

Resist the urge to do everything for your children. The real world will not cater to their every whim and desire, nor should you. Even the youngest of children can be incorporated into some of our daily tasks, whether it's meal prep, setting the table, helping with dishes or laundry, feeding the pets, watering the plants, or whatever you and your husband have on your long to-do list. Once they are able to safely carry a dish over to the sink, insist they clean up after themselves after each meal. Ditto for putting away their own laundry. With both parents working full-time in most homes today, you need every spare moment you can get. Not to mention, you do them no favors by waiting on them hand and foot. Their future roommates aren't going to pick up the slack if they leave their dishes in the sink or leave a pile of clothes in the middle of their bedroom floor. Preparing them to live independently in the real world is one of the most important jobs a parent has in raising their children. If your daughter has been coddled and waited on throughout her childhood, she is in for a rude awakening when she leaves home absent her maid and personal assistant.

When it comes to spiritual training, the pre-launch phase should be used to build a foundation of faith in your daughter's lives. Teach her to love God's Word and to communicate with God through prayer. Pray with her and let her get comfortable praying out loud. Teach her basic biblical truths and reinforce that teaching by plugging into a Bible-believing local church. Attend consistently.

Make it a higher priority than sports or extracurricular activities that may fall on Sundays. I cannot stress the importance of cultivating this discipline and modeling for your daughters a deep reliance on gathering with a fellowship of believers. Iron sharpens iron, and your daughters will need all the reinforcement they can get to prepare them to live in the world without becoming of the world (Rom. 12:2).

Test Launch: The stage of a daughter's life from age fourteen to eighteen should be viewed as the test launch phase. Your daughter should be becoming more independent as she exercises the key life skills. During this stage she will have to learn some painful lessons as you begin to wean her from dependence on you and give her ownership and personal responsibility. Many moms have a tendency to come to the rescue of their children and bail them out of consequences from sinful or poor decisions. Moms need to allow their daughters to learn the higher lesson by refusing to rescue them from the consequences that may result. In the real world no one will rescue them from consequences that come as a result of laziness and irresponsibility. For example, when each of our children began driving at sixteen, my husband was clear on the expectations of car ownership. They were given used cars and told they would have to earn money for gas. We paid for the insurance, but we made clear that if they received a ticket or had an accident, they had to pay for the ticket, defensive driving course, and any amount required to repair the vehicle. But that's not all. We also told them they would have to pay any subsequent monthly increase in our insurance premium that resulted from their ticket/accident or lose the car.

My younger son (seventeen at the time) was issued a speeding ticket and experienced the pain of watching over more than one hundred dollars disappear from his savings account to pay for an online defensive driving course to cover the ticket and prevent the insurance premium from increasing. He had a minor fender-bender shortly thereafter that left his back bumper slightly dented with the paint rubbed off and was unable to afford to have it repaired. We also did not nag or remind him about taking the online defensive driving course. If he didn't have the incentive to follow through, we were prepared to follow through by drawing the amount needed from his savings account to cover the ticket and subsequent increase in insurance.

Once your daughter is sixteen, if she is able to balance a part-time job, consider having her work to earn her leisure money or gas money. She is also old enough to make her own appointments whether it be for a haircut or dentist/doctor appointment. Have her fill out her own paperwork when required. Prepare her to maintain a budget and give her a few financial responsibilities. My youngest child participated in a Dave Ramsey Financial Peace program (daveramsey.com) during his high school years, and I highly recommend his materials which span from age three and up. By the time your daughter reaches the test launch phase, she should be putting some of these financial disciplines into practice.

When it comes to spiritual disciplines, your daughter should be able to pray on her own, initiate time alone with God, and participate in projects that serve others (mission trips, community outreach projects, etc.). During this phase, some parents allow their teenagers to decide whether or not they will attend church and be involved in youth group activities. My husband and I felt strongly that as long as our children lived under our roof, they would be required to follow our guidelines and thus, attend church and be involved in the youth group, as well as take a few mission trips.

Final Launch: The stage of a girl's life from age eighteen to twenty-two should be viewed as the final launch phase. At some point during this stage a daughter should become independent of her parents and become a responsible member of society. While some parents may hold the view that age eighteen signals true adulthood, others may feel it is a bit older, especially if college is a part of the plan. Regardless of whether you aim for eighteen or twenty-two, anything much older than twenty-two will increase the chances of a failure to launch. Dr. Leonard Sax notes:

> My own belief, based in part on my twenty years of medical practice, is that if parents continue to shelter their adult child after the age of twenty-one years, the parents may make it less likely that the adult child will ever be willing and able to meet the challenges of the real world.[1]

Prior to the final launch, parents should help their children project the future and weigh the possibilities, all the while making the objective clear: *You need to be independent by the age of* ___ (whatever age you determine is reasonable). Some children are not cut out for college and would perhaps do better with vocational training. Vocational training is making a comeback as society realizes that many young people lack the funds and/or ambition to attend college. In addition, there is a demand for many specialty vocations that don't require a college degree. A *Time* magazine article entitled "Grow Up? Not So Fast," reported a surge in apprenticeship programs that give high school graduates a cheaper and more practical alternative to college.

> In 1996 Jack Smith, then CEO of General Motors, started Automotive Youth Educational Systems (AYES), a program that puts high school kids in shops alongside seasoned car mechanics. More than 7,800 students have tried it, and 98 percent of them have ended up working at the business

where they apprenticed. "I knew this was my best way to get into a dealership," says Chris Rolando, 20, an AYES graduate who works at one in Detroit. "My friends are still at pizza-place jobs and have no idea what to do for a living. I just bought my own house and have a career."[2]

If you recognize in advance that your daughter is not a candidate for college and would be better suited for a vocational career, it's not a bad idea to expose her to training opportunities by the age of sixteen, while she is still under your roof. One friend of mine who has three children required each one to learn a trained vocational skill in their late high school years in addition to their college education that followed. I thought this was a wonderful idea and wish I had thought to do this with my own children as a back-up plan to make them more marketable in a tough economy. All three of my children ended up attending college but not without clear expectations set forth as to what we expected as a return on our investment. In fact, my husband drew up a contract for each of our three children and required them to sign it before we would agree to send them to college. While we required our children to work in the summer months and earn money toward some college expenses, we paid for the bulk of their college expenses and made it clear that in doing so their college education was a privilege and not a right. They knew that if they did not fulfill their end of the contract, the funding for college would cease.

In the contract my husband detailed what exactly we would cover over a four-year period. Should they not finish in a four-year period, they would need to secure a loan to pay for the remainder of their college education. My oldest son graduated (in four and a half years) and, as per the contract agreement, secured a loan (on his own) to pay for the last semester. He also had to cover tuition, books, and living expenses. The contract also required that each child take a minimum of fifteen hours/semester; earn a minimum GPA (determined based on each child's academic potential); remain consistently involved in a local church and Bible study while in college; and involvement in wholesome extracurricular activities, such as Christian clubs and intramural sports. If they flunked a course, they were required to pay us back the entire amount for the course.

I realize this may seem harsh to some reading this, but my husband and I are of the school of thought that college educations are a privilege, not a right, and college is not a season of life where young people are supposed to "sow their wild oats." For the amount we invested in their college education, we had every right to attach strings to our offer.

In addition, we made it clear that upon graduating from college, they could return home, but only as a transition to the next step in their employment time line. We likened it to a "layover" at an airport where they might need a little time at the gate (find a job, apartment, etc.) before they embarked on their final destination—adulthood!

Mission Accomplished

As mothers, our hearts are wired to nurture and care for our children. When they are young and utterly dependent on us to have their needs met, we feel a sense of value and worth. It feels good to be *needed*. We must remember that our divine call as mothers is to raise up godly seed for the next generation. And part of "raising 'em up" is to "move 'em out." Or "cut the cord," so to speak. It is unbiblical to allow our children to remain dependent on us after they reach a reasonable age of self-sufficiency. It is God's design for children to become adults while under the tutelage of their parents.

Even if you are getting a late start, I encourage you to develop a launch plan for your children. When I introduced the concept of developing a launch plan in my original version of this book, my children were all still in the nest. I guess you could say the jury was out regarding whether or not our launch plan would prove to be effective. As I write this update nearly a decade after including our launch plan in the original version of this book, I have witnessed firsthand the benefits. All three of my children have since graduated from college (in 4–4.5 years), secured full-time jobs shortly after graduation, married wonderful and godly spouses (by age twenty-two), became first-time parents (by ages twenty-three to twenty-six) diligently saved for a down payment for a home and were all first-time home owners by the age of twenty-five. Most importantly, they (along with their spouses) love the Lord and are committed to raising their children to love and follow God. My husband and I could not be more proud of them. We made plenty of mistakes along the way and weren't always consistent in our training, but God more than made up for our lack. I share that to say, hang in there!

Your children may not thank you now for a tough love approach that encourages them to grow up, but one day, hopefully you'll get the thanks you deserve. At the very least, you can expect to hear a "well done good and faithful servant!" from God.

Chapter 12

It's Okay to Dream about Marriage and Motherhood

● ● ● ● ● ●

Delight yourself in the LORD, and he will give
you the desires of your heart. (Ps. 37:4 ESV)

When my daughter was young, like many other little girls, she loved playing house. If we had friends over with young sons, there was a high likelihood they would be recruited to play the part of the groom in a staged mock wedding. She would fetch her pint-size pretend wedding gown and veil out of her dress-up box and stage a mock wedding on the spot. After a quick walk down the aisle, these lucky lads were thrust instantly into fatherhood and forced to help care for their fast-growing family of stuffed animals and dolls. Without any coaxing on the part of my husband or myself, marriage and motherhood was on her radar. It was natural for her to dream about someday taking that walk down the aisle and beginning a real family.

While I acknowledge that not all girls grow up dreaming about marriage and motherhood, I think it's fair to say that most do. Marriage and parenthood have always been viewed as benchmarks of adulthood, but unfortunately both have been on the decline for years. Consider that in 1980, the US Census Bureau reported that less than 5 percent of women had never been married by age forty-five. In 2015, that number had increased to 17 percent.[1] A report released by Demographic Intelligence, which tracks marriage and birth trends in the United States, said marriage rates are the lowest in a century and are projected to decline even more over the next decade.[2] In 2017, the average age of first marriage in for women was 27.4 and for men, 29.5. Compare this to 1965 when it was 20.6 for women and 22.8 for men.[3] As cohabitation and having children outside of marriage have become more socially acceptable, marriage as an institution is no longer viewed as a necessity.

Even more disturbing, surveys indicate that there has been a shift in the priorities among today's teens and young adults when they consider their long-term life goals. Consider that in 1976, Boomer high school seniors rated "having a good marriage and family life" higher than any other life goal. By 2011, marriage and family had slipped to fourth (behind finding steady work, being successful at work, and "giving my children better opportunities than I had." Marriage and family remained at fourth in 2015, as well.[4] According to author, Jean Twenge, "marriage and children are just not as high on iGen's priority list."[5] In fact, in a recent Barna survey of today's teens and young adults (iGen or Gen Z), only 20 percent listed "getting married" as a goal they wanted to accomplish before the age of thirty. Only 12 percent desire to "become a parent" by age thirty. This was a sharp decrease from the 20 percent of Millennials who desire to "become a parent" by age thirty.[6] Should this lack of a desire to marry and have children hold, I predict we will see many who choose not to have children at all or to have only one child. Birth rates are already on the decline supporting this likely trajectory.

The trend of delayed marriage and parenthood will have a direct impact on the ever-increasing population of single adults, increased infertility issues among women, and even the role grandparents play in helping their adult children. All it takes is two generations who delay having children into their thirties to put the average age of first-time grandparents into their sixties to seventies. This is not talked about often, but as a first-time grandparent at the age of forty-eight who is now in my mid-fifties (with five grandkids and counting!), I grieve over the devastating impact this will have on the ability of grandparents to be actively involved in their grandchildren's growing up years, as well as help their adult children during a time when they need it most. Many will not live long enough to see their grandchildren graduate from high school, much less attend their weddings. This is not just sad for a generation of grandparents, but also for the grandchildren who will miss the blessing of this special relationship.

Marriage and motherhood are not things you enter into lightly, and this chapter is certainly not intended to be a propaganda campaign to suggest that all girls are destined to marry and have children. Some women will willingly choose to remain single, while others may find themselves unwilling victims of circumstance. Not every girl will go on to marry and have children, but a whopping majority will. For that reason, I felt it necessary to include some critical information to pass along to your daughters should they be among those who have marriage and motherhood on their "someday" radars.

Theologian and author R. Albert Mohler Jr. offered this reminder about marriage:

> Christians see marriage, first of all, as an institution
> made good and holy by the Creator. Its value, for us, is
> not established by sociology but by Scripture. We also
> understand that God gave us marriage for our good, for
> our protection, for our sanctification, and for human
> flourishing. In other words, the Bible compels us to see
> marriage as essential to human happiness, health, and
> infinitely more.[7]

In order to be advocates for marriage, we must first identify the primary threats that seek to undermine God's design and purpose for marriage and threaten to rob the next generation of "human happiness, health, and infinitely more." It is imperative that we are intentional in teaching our daughters God's view and intent for marriage, rather than allow the mind-set of the culture to influence their thinking. I find it ironic that studies are revealing that the current generation of children and teens are reporting record level increases in loneliness due, no doubt, to the increase in shallow, virtual relationships in place of real emotional intimacy. God created marriage to reduce our aloneness. Yes, it requires hard work, but the payoff to having someone to share life's greatest joys with (as well as sorrows) cannot be matched by any other substitute. Marriage was intended by God to bring "health and human happiness," but our culture has perpetuated the lie that it is the very hindrance to "health and human happiness." Do your daughters believe this lie?

Cheap Sex

Mark Regenerus, socialogist and author of the book *Cheap Sex: The Transformation of Men, Marriage, and Monogamy* believes that cheap sex has doomed the institution of marriage. He claims that with porn on-demand and greater reproductive freedom, sex is a commodity that is available at any time and has left men with little motivation for marriage.[8] Women used to have leverage when they would require marriage before sex, but with the onset of sex as a free and recreational hobby, men no longer have incentive to "grow up" and get married. It brings to mind an old saying common in our grandparents' day, "Why buy the cow if you can get the milk for free?" Regnerus goes on to argue that "men are in the driver's seat in the marriage market and are optimally positioned to navigate it in a way that privileges their (sexual) interests and preferences. It need not even be conscious behavior on their part."[9]

In chapter 7, I discussed the irony in encouraging our children to save themselves for marriage while also endorsing delayed marriage. Of course, it's *possible* to remain pure until your late twenties (or older), but is it *likely?* William Doherty, director of the Marriage and Family Therapy Program at the University of Minnesota, agrees that a contradictory message is being sent to our children when we preach abstinence and, at the same time, expose them to societal pressures to delay marriage. "From a traditional moral and religious standpoint, if you want to discourage premarital sex, you really need to be encouraging earlier marriage," he advises.[10] As a disclaimer, he is not endorsing teenage marriages, noting they are risky. He makes the point that "when you get into your twenties, those teen risks go away."[11]

In a thought-provoking essay addressing the problem of stunted maturity among men, author Frederica Mathewes-Green states that "God designed our bodies to desire to mate much earlier, and through most of history cultures have accommodated that desire by enabling people to wed by their late teens or early twenties. People would postpone marriage until their late twenties only in cases of economic disaster or famine—times when people had to save up in order to marry."[12] Again, I am not a proponent of teenage marriages, but I do think we need to be honest with our daughters when it comes to the delayed marriage. The irony is that many young people delay marriage in an attempt to reduce the chance of divorce, yet in reality they actually increase their chances of experiencing a failed marriage! Mathewes-Green notes that "fifty years ago, when the average bride was twenty, the divorce rate was half what it is now, because the culture encouraged and sustained marriage."[13]

Can you imagine the impact on the average age of marriage if girls refused to hook up or cohabitate and rather made clear they were saving sex for marriage? As one twenty-eight-year-old man told the author of a book on marriage: "If I had to be married to have sex, I would probably be married, as would every guy I know."[14] What an interesting bit of insight over the moral mess that has resulted from hooking up and cohabitation. So much for the sexual revolution that sought to bring women the same sexual freedoms as men, with no marital strings attached. In the end women are more beholden to men than ever as their biological clocks tick away while the men pursue free sex with no obligation to commit further.

Please don't misunderstand—I am certainly not laying blame for the problems associated with delayed marriage solely on women. There is equal blame to go around. Nor am I suggesting we manip-ulate our daughters into marrying at a younger age. I am simply calling this issue to your attention in an effort to note the importance of relying on God's wisdom rather than blindly subscribing to the faulty wisdom of the world. We have a responsibility to teach our daughters to look to God for direction, rather than blindly follow the culture's lead. Part of launching our daughters into adulthood is raising them to have a biblical mind-set about marriage.

Shacking Up

While many Christian parents are failing to talk with their adolescent/teenage children about the importance of saving sex for marriage, even more are failing to talk about cohabitation. For many parents it doesn't even make the radar until after their children leave home and they are faced with the reality of the situation when it occurs. Like a minister's wife I know, whose son recently dropped the bomb that he would be moving in with his girlfriend because "times have changed" and "everyone does that now." Both her son and his girlfriend had been involved in Christian ministry in their college years and even mentored high school students. They knew better, but chose to conform to the world rather than abide by God's order and design for marriage.

For this reason we must be devoted to discussing the impact of cohabitation with our children before they leave the nest. We must not be naive to believe they will not succumb to the pressures of the day. Since 1960 the number of unmarried couples who live together has increased more than tenfold.[15] What was considered immoral and unacceptable fifty years ago has now shifted to become somewhat of an expectation, especially among men. The study by the National Marriage Project found that most of the participants view cohabitation in a favorable light, and almost all the men agreed with the view that a man should not marry a woman until he has lived with her first.[16] Nearly 70 percent of those who get married lived together first.[17]

So, what is the appeal or the reasoning behind the decision to shack up? The study above sheds light on the three most common reasons cited by unmarried singles in the study above:[18]

They hope to find out more about the habits, character, and fidelity of a partner.

They want to test compatibility, possibly for future marriage.

They want to live together as a way of avoiding the risks of divorce or being "trapped in an unhappy marriage."

There seems to be much confusion and miscommunication regarding any "perceived" benefits of cohabitation. Ironically cohabitation actually increases the risk that the relationship will break up before marriage. A National Marriage Project report states that "many studies have found that those who live together before marriage have less satisfying marriages and a considerably higher chance of eventually breaking up." One reason is that people who cohabit may be more skittish of commitment and more likely to call it quits when problems arise. Additionally the act of living together may lead to attitudes that make happy marriages more difficult. The findings of one recent study, for example, suggest, "There may be less motivation for cohabitating partners to develop their conflict resolution and support skills."[19] Those who do go on to marry have higher separation and divorce rates.[20] And whether they go on to marry their cohabitation partner or someone else, they are more likely to have extramarital affairs. When it comes to staying faithful, married partners have higher rates of loyalty every time. One study done over a five-year period, reported in Sexual Attitudes and Lifestyles, indicates 90 percent of married women were monogamous compared to 60 percent of cohabiting women. Statistics were even more dramatic with male faithfulness: 90 percent of married men remained true to their brides, while only 43 percent of cohabiting men stayed true to their partners.[21] Additionally those who choose cohabitation under the assumption that the sex will be better than "married" sex should take note: According to a large-scale national study, *married people have both more and better sex than do their unmarried counterparts*. Not only do they have sex more often, but they enjoy it more, both physically and emotionally.[22]

Our daughters deserve to know the truth when it comes to the risks associated with cohabitation. Not only is it out of the will of God, it is threat to their future health and happiness in marriage.

The Good News No One's Talking About

Marriage is not doomed, but it is in danger. The good news is that 77 percent of twelfth graders in 2015 said they "expect to marry," which is exactly the same percent of Boomers who claimed the same in 1976.[23] Unfortunately our young people will hear little about the benefits of marriage. When was the last time you heard the media address the overwhelming and consistent findings by such reputable sources as *The Journal of Marriage and the Family* and the *American Journal of Sociology* that "married persons, both men and women, are on average considerably better off than all categories of unmarried persons (never married, divorced, separated, and widowed) in terms of happiness, satisfaction, physical health, longevity, and most aspects of emotional health?"[24] Given that God created marriage, should it really come as a surprise that marriage is, in fact, good for us?

Mothers, it's up to us to extol the benefits of marriage to our daughters as a God-ordained union that can bring much happiness and, most important, honor to Him. The National Marriage Project states that the burden of changing attitudes about marriage rests with parents. "Contrary to the popular notion that the media is chiefly responsible for young people's attitudes about mating and marriage, available evidence strongly suggests that young people get many of their ideas and models of marriage from parents and the parental generation.[25] That's the good news. The bad news is that the same study also found that "many parents have had almost nothing good to say about marriage and often say nothing at all," claiming the negativism and/or silence could be due to "the parental generation's own marital problems and failures."[26]

Further, when polling young people about their attitudes regarding marriage, many in the study have unfortunately grown up with unhappily married or divorced parents. They have no baseline for determining what a healthy marriage even looks like and have therefore been left with a tainted picture. Some even described a good marriage as "the opposite of my parents."[27] Ouch. Moreover, a number of participants in the study said they received "no advice" or "mainly negative advice" about marriage from their "parents and relatives."[28] How can we break the chains of this dysfunctional cycle when many are, in fact, perpetuating and encouraging it? No doubt some of you reading this have experienced your fair share of hurt and pain in marriage. Most failed marriages can be traced back to a failure on the part of one or both spouses to adhere to God's standards of marriage. When these standards are not followed, marriages can suffer and sometimes even fail. If this is your case, can you accept responsibility for your mistakes and still speak highly about the institution of marriage when talking to your daughters? Of course, if you are a Christian who is married to an unbeliever, you can point out to your daughter God's counsel for Christians not to be "unequally yoked" (2 Cor. 6:14). (This needs to be done in a manner that would not dishonor your husband.) God can heal any marriage, and prayer is an essential part of that process.

The problem is that too many with broken marriages are claiming marriage, in general, is the mistake. We must distinguish that God doesn't create mistakes, but people, in fact, make mistakes. I realize others may be reading this who followed God's standards and, for whatever reason, your once godly husband chose to walk away or chase after a life of sin. I personally know several women who experienced this painful misfortune, and it is heartbreaking. Even though they have had a sour experience, they have not allowed the experience to sour their attitudes regarding marriage. They have worked hard to speak highly of marriage and make sure their children are not left with a negative impression of marriage.

For those of us who currently have healthy marriages, have we done our part in talking up marriage in the hearing of our children? Do they know how much we value marriage? Do they see us exhibit affection and swap caring words? Do they witness positive examples of conflict/resolution and confession/forgiveness? Trust me, I am personally convicted by the weight of those words. I love being married. Sure, it's tough at times, and my husband and I have had our fair share of bumps along the way, but I wouldn't trade it for anything. Marriage is a gift from God. Moms, if we want to see a new PR campaign for marriage take place, it will start in our own homes . . . beginning with us.

Delayed Marriage and Declining Fertility

Another challenge our daughters will face when it comes to marriage and motherhood is the trend of delayed marriage. While at first glance it may appear to be harmless, it, in truth, has far-reaching effects on our daughters. They will be the ones to come up with the short-end of the stick. As their biological clocks tick away, their single male friends experience no external pressures to wed. The single males have their pick of a sea of women (including much younger) who are bidding for their attention. The National Marriage Project report concludes, "If this trend continues, it will not be good news for the many young women who hope to marry and bear children before they begin to face problems associated with declining fertility."[29]

Is it any wonder that the number of unmarried women between the ages of thirty and thirty-four has more than tripled during the past thirty years and that the percentage of childless women in their early forties has doubled?[30] Wendy Shalit, author of the book *Girls Gone Mild*, describes this cruel irony: "Single women approaching their late twenties become more serious about the search for a marriage partner. They've gained confidence in their capacity to 'make it on their own,' and they are ready to think about marriage. However, many say the 'men aren't there,' they're 'not on the same page,' or they're less mature."[31]

No wonder the waiting rooms of fertility clinics are bursting at the seams with women in their thirties and forties who were led to believe they had nothing to worry about. We don't see the heartache behind those visits, the tears shed over a failed procedure, or the endless shots and pills that are required, not to mention the money spent for a shot-in-the-dark chance at motherhood. No, instead, we continue to see the lucky ones who have the money at their disposal to increase their luck even further. No wonder so many women are bitter when they discover the truth . . . the hard way.

In addition to other factors I have discussed prior to this chapter that can lead to delayed marriage (hooking up, cohabitation, sexual promiscuity leading to STDs), we must also add this one to the list—the purposeful postponement of marriage and motherhood for the sake of career-building. Albert Mohler, president of Southern Baptist Theological Seminary and host of a nationwide radio show "devoted to engaging contemporary culture with the biblical truth," had this to say in a blog on the topic: "To a considerable extent, the fertility crisis for women is a crisis of delayed marriage and delayed motherhood. Women have been sold a lie— that they can have it all. The hard reality is that none of us, male or female, can have it all."[32]

In a *New York Times* editorial piece addressing the problem of infertility due to delayed marriage and motherhood, Dr. Zev Rosenwaks, the director of The Center for Reproductive Medicine and Infertility had this to say:

> The non-stop media parade of midlife women producing offspring is stunning. . . . These stories are about the fortunate ones: they beat the odds. . . . As an infertility specialist, I often see women . . . who have been lulled into a mistaken belief that there is a medical technology that will allow women to have their genetic children whenever they choose. . . . In our eagerness to outwit time, the media have made a bestseller out of the freshly minted fiction of "rewinding the biological clock." We can't and we haven't.[33]

The former director of RESOLVE, a support network for couples coping with infertility, reports: "I can't tell you how many people we've had on our help line, crying and saying they had no idea how much fertility drops as you age."[34] Yet many of these same women are likely knowledgeable about the preventive measures you can take to avoid contracting osteoporosis or skin cancer! Not that there hasn't been an attempt to get the word out to young women regarding factors that can lead to infertility.

Consider the following facts:

- If you are a healthy thirty-year-old woman, you have about a 20 percent chance per month to get pregnant. By age forty, however, your chance is only about 5 percent per month.[35]

- At age thirty-nine the chance of a live birth after an IVF attempt is 8 percent. By age forty-four, it falls to 3 percent.[36]

- The actual rate for successful birth using frozen eggs is closer to 2.5 percent.[37]

- If a woman conceives at age thirty-eight, the possibility of miscarriage has tripled, the rate of stillbirth has doubled, and the risk of genetic abnormality is six times as great.[38] Additionally, the pregnancy is more likely to be complicated by high blood pressure or diabetes, and the baby is more likely to be premature or low birth weight.[39]

- Women treated for infertility suffer from anxiety and depression as severely as patients who have been diagnosed with cancer or cardiac disease.[40]

I can vouch for the validity of that last statistic after watching my daughter and son-in-law struggle with infertility for nearly three years. Granted, my daughter was only twenty-two years old when they began trying to start family. After one year with no luck, they found themselves sitting in a fertility clinic and hearing a diagnosis no couple wants to hear: "Unexplained Infertility." For the next two years plus, my daughter endured a battery of tests and multiple procedures all to no avail. They moved on to more invasive procedures like IUI and eventually IVF, each month watching their hope (and savings) dwindle with every negative result. It was heart-wrenching as a mother to see my daughter wrestle with the "what-ifs." She had dreamed of becoming a mother since she was a little girl and never imagined it would be so difficult, especially since she was so young. Finally, on IVF transfer #5, they received the good news they had longed to hear month after month after month. Given the failure rate after four failed IVF transfers, my granddaughter, Molly Grace is a miracle. Molly means "wished for child," and that is an understatement to say the least!

Many of our girls are buying the lie that marriage and motherhood can be postponed indefinitely. The culture has shouted, "You can have it all!" and they actually believed it. Like my daughter learned during her battle with infertility, dreams can't always be scheduled on a preferred and pre-scheduled timeline. No one tells the other part of the story when it comes to delayed marriage. We hear nothing about the difficulties that arise when adjusting to marriage after years spent single and unencumbered. We hear nothing about the impact the number of sexual partners has on the health of a marriage on down the road. We hear nothing about the heartache that arises when problems of infertility surface. And we hear nothing about the exhaustion that comes from raising children at an age when many of our own parents were gearing up for retirement.

And then there are the dear Christian women who wanted nothing more than to be married and start a family in their twenties, but unexpectedly found themselves in their thirties and forties single and/or childless, unwilling victims of the delayed marriage trend. Our churches are bursting at the seams with this fast-growing segment of the population and scrambling to minister to their unique needs.

Telling Our Daughters the Truth

What is a mother to tell her daughter? Certainly, we don't tell her to settle for the first young man who looks her way. Nor am I suggesting that we manipulate God's timing regarding marriage. At the very least, we owe it to our daughters to tell them the truth. If marriage and motherhood are something they dream about, it may be wise for them to think twice about putting it on a back burner when it comes to their future life goals. For some girls, it will not be in God's will for them to marry. For yet others God may choose to delay marriage. Our daughters need to know that God's timing works best when we abide by His timetable rather than our own. Romans 12:2 reminds us, "Don't copy the behavior and customs of this world, but let God transform you into a new person by changing the way you think. Then you will learn to know God's will for you, which is good and pleasing and perfect" (NLT). Whether marriage is part of God's plan for your daughter or not, she needs to know that the most important relationship she will ever have is her relationship with Jesus Christ. When she makes her relationship with Christ the focus, everything else will fall into place. Marriage may or may not be a part of her future, but if her eyes are on Jesus and her heart beats first and foremost for Him, the outcome won't matter.

Talk about It

· · · · · · · · · · ·

Chapter 10

Why do you think many children and youth today show little interest in becoming adults?

How might have parents contributed to the problem of delayed adolescence?

Were you surprised to find out that kids today are safer than previous generations? Why then, do you feel parents today have a tendency to overprotect and coddle their children?

What steps do you feel led to take to better prepare your daughter for adulthood?

Chapter 11

Do you have a launch plan for your daughter to help her transition for girlhood to womanhood? Would you say she is on track?

Is your daughter in the pre-launch, test launch, or final launch phase? What are some steps you are currently taking to increase her level of responsibility and prepare her for the future? If you are not currently taking steps, what steps do you plan to take?

Write down below a vision for what it would look like to achieve a status of "mission accomplished" for your daughter and by what age.

In what areas did you feel ill-prepared when you launched into adulthood? How might this impact your launch plan for your daughter?

Chapter 12

Were you surprised to find out that today's generation shows a declining interest in marriage and parenthood?

What is your view of marriage? Is it overall positive, indifferent, or negative? How do you think your view has impacted your daughter's view of marriage?

Does your daughter view marriage and motherhood as part of her future?

Have you ever discussed with your daughter the ways cohabitation can have an effect on future marriage?

What about the impact of delayed marriage on fertility?

Do you believe your daughter has bought into the lie that she can "have it all"?

Conversation 5

You are who you've been becoming.

Chapter 13

Who Can Find a Virtuous Woman?

● ● ● ● ● ●

*Who can find a virtuous woman? For her price
is far above rubies. (Prov. 31:10 KJV)*

I've heard plenty of stories firsthand from mothers over the years who can attest to the moral free-fall we are seeing in the current culture. Little surprises me at this point, but I was taken aback recently when a mother of a middle school daughter shared that parents at her daughter's school were alerted by school administrators that some of the girls were selling nude photos to the boys at school. Let that sink in for a minute. We're talking about 7th and 8th grade boys (ages twelve to fourteen) offering 7th and 8th grade girls money for topless and fully nude pictures. Wondering if this was an unfortunate and isolated event, I posted about it on social media and asked mothers of middle school daughters if they thought this was happening at their daughters' schools. Sure enough, other mothers chimed in that similar stories were emerging at their schools.

Our daughters are growing up in a culture where "bad" has become the new "good." It brings to mind the question posed in Proverbs 31:10 "Who can find a virtuous woman? for her price is far above rubies" (KJV). Today, virtue is a scarcely used word thought by many to be an outdated concept of days past. Why opt for *virtue* when you can have *empowerment*? To possess virtue, you must strive for moral excellence, which in turn, holds you accountable to a standard of right and wrong. Empowerment, on the other hand, is most often connected to the word "self" which more adequately reveals its true mission—self-empowerment. It's all about ME! Self rules! With empowerment, anything goes because you have the power to choose your own standard of morality.

Seems I recall our dear sister Eve buying into the lie of empowerment. With one bite of the forbidden fruit, the serpent said her eyes would be opened and opened they were—to a new concept called "good and evil." With this new knowledge, she hoped to gain power, yet in the end, was left power-less. She was snared by what has become Satan's oldest trick in the book: The focus on self. The enemy knows what many of us have had to learn the hard way: When the focus is on self, it is off God. Today, women are no different. Empowerment sounds so alluring. It promises to fulfill our innermost needs. In its most radical form it sends damaging messages to women of all ages. If you desire to climb to the top of the career ladder, yet it would require you to sacrifice your family on the altar of success, big deal! It's all about *you*! Why wait to have sex until you're married? Empowerment has no rules except "if it feels good do it." "Look out for #1 and run roughshod over anyone who tries to get in your way."

Our young girls have been thoroughly indoctrinated into the pre-empowerment, "girl power" movement. It is peddled to girls through fashion magazines, television, movies, music, and advertisements. The movement encourages them to be the aggressors in relationships, to pursue success at any cost, to dress any way they please, and to have sex with whomever they want whenever they want with no strings attached. Sex has become recreational, having been downgraded from sacred to secular. They are taught to trample over anyone who might hinder them from worshipping almighty "self." Whereas virtue encourages the pursuit of moral excellence, empowerment seeks to dominate and conquer. It is harsh, abrasive, and altogether unattractive. It is strength misused for purposes that are null and void of any meaning.

We have the answer. We know the One who truly, liberates. Jesus Christ liberated women some 2,000 years ago, when He cried out on the cross, "It is finished." True strength comes in knowing Jesus Christ. He is the only one who can satisfy a restless heart. He is the source of strength for the virtuous woman. In fact, if you take a closer look at that word "virtuous" in Proverbs 31:10, you'll find a brand of strength that far exceeds the strength peddled by the culture.

One Bible commentary defined *virtue* as "moral courage."[1] I realize that many women may be somewhat hesitant to embrace the concept that a virtuous woman could have a feisty side to her when it comes to fighting for noble causes. In fact, I was amazed to discover that the actual Hebrew word used for "virtuous" in Proverbs 31:10, "Who can find a virtuous woman?" is *chayil*. It is used a total of 243 times in the Old Testament. Only three times of the 243 times the word appears is the English word "virtuous" used in its place. Most often when *chayil* is used, it is substituted for translation purposes most often with the English words, "army" (56 times) and "valour" or "valiant" (50 times). Other English words substituted for the word *chayil* are host, forces, power, might, strength, and strong. One verse where "chayil" is used is in 1 Samuel 16:18. It speaks of David before he became king and says:

One of the servants answered, "I have seen a son of Jesse of Bethlehem who knows how to play the harp. He is a brave man and a warrior [chayil]" (1 Sam 16:18a NIV).

A virtuous woman is a strong, mighty, and valiant force. She is a warrior for righteousness. She would never settle for the world's counterfeit brand of strength called empowerment. Her strength comes from God and not herself. To give you a bit of a background on the Proverbs 31 passage, it is speculated that King Lemuel wrote the verses as he reflected on his mother's teaching regarding the type of wife he should seek. Theologians believe that the poem did not originate with King Lemuel's mother but was rather, a free-standing poem that had been passed down for many generations for the purpose of aiding men in identifying an ideal wife, as well as giving women a formula for becoming a virtuous woman. The twenty-two verses are in an acrostic format with each verse beginning with consecutive letters of the Hebrew alphabet to aid in easy memorization. By looking to Proverbs 31, we see an idea of the type of woman (young and old) who is esteemed in the eyes of God. While at first glance the passage may appear to be an outdated fixture of the past, the Proverbs 31 woman's character qualities stand the test of time. As you read the beautiful passage below, attempt to look past her actions and focus instead on the condition of her heart and the over-arching character qualities that define a virtuous woman.

¹⁰ Who can find a virtuous woman?

For her price is far above rubies.

¹¹ The heart of her husband doth safely trust in her,

So that he shall have no need of spoil.

¹² She will do him good and not evil

All the days of her life.

¹³ She seeketh wool, and flax,

And worketh willingly with her hands.

¹⁴ She is like the merchants' ships;

She bringeth her food from afar.

¹⁵ She riseth also while it is yet night,

And giveth meat to her household,

And a portion to her maidens.

¹⁶ She considereth a field, and buyeth it:

With the fruit of her hands she planteth a vineyard.

¹⁷ She girdeth her loins with strength,

And strengtheneth her arms.

¹⁸ She perceiveth that her merchandise is good:

Her candle goeth not out by night.

¹⁹ She layeth her hands to the spindle,

And her hands hold the distaff.

²⁰ She stretcheth out her hand to the poor;

Yea, she reacheth forth her hands to the needy.

²¹ She is not afraid of the snow for her household:

For all her household are clothed with scarlet.

²² She maketh herself coverings of tapestry;

Her clothing is silk and purple.

²³ Her husband is known in the gates,

When he sitteth among the elders of the land.

²⁴ She maketh fine linen, and selleth it;

And delivereth girdles unto the merchant.

²⁵ Strength and honour are her clothing;

And she shall rejoice in time to come.

²⁶ She openeth her mouth with wisdom;

And in her tongue is the law of kindness.

²⁷ She looketh well to the ways of her household,

And eateth not the bread of idleness.

²⁸ Her children arise up, and call her blessed;

Her husband also, and he praiseth her.

²⁹ Many daughters have done virtuously,

But thou excellest them all.

³⁰ Favour is deceitful, and beauty is vain:

But a woman that feareth the Lord, she shall be praised.

³¹ Give her of the fruit of her hands;

And let her own works praise her in the gates. (KJV)

All too often, this passage is taught to encourage Christian women to emulate this woman's specific behaviors (with an emphasis on the domestic ones) rather than focusing on her heart. While the culture is guilty of peddling a false brand of strength and empowerment to women, sadly, many Christians have undersold (or altogether ignored) the strength and empowerment God intended for women. I've heard teaching over the years related to the Proverbs 31 passage used to guilt women who work outside the home, fail to keep a tidy home, and everything in between. Yet, a closer look at this passage tells a completely different story. No doubt, she was fiercely devoted to her family, putting their needs above her own. But don't mistake this woman as a subservient doormat of a wife whose sole identity is found in being a wife, mother, and homemaker.

As we dissect the passage with an emphasis on the condition of her heart rather than her specific behaviors, we see many character qualities emerge that set her apart from the average woman. We find that she was extremely selfless and put the needs of others (her family, servants, the poor and needy) before her own. She was pleasant to be around—thinking before she speaks, kind and compassionate to all. She was a hard worker—efficient and resourceful, not one to waste time or resources. She was strong in body and spirit, and not one to succumb to idleness. She was selfless and attentive not only to her family, but also the needs of the poor and needy. She was confident and content—not worried for about the future, whatever it may hold. She was wise not only in her speech, but also with her money. She was independent and even entrepreneurial—developing skills to earn money and make investments. She was confident in her reflection in the mirror and not taken to issues of vanity. (Ouch!) Most importantly, she was praised for her defining quality—a devotion to God above all else.

The Conclusion of the Matter

In verse 30 of the Proverbs 31 passage, we discover the source of the virtuous woman's strength. Her ability to "fear the Lord" was the key factor that set her apart from other women. Verse 30 reminds us that "charm is deceptive, and beauty is fleeting; but a woman who fears the Lord is to be praised." King Solomon was someone who was known for possessing great wisdom. He had personally reaped the benefits of wealth, knowledge, and power; yet he continued to question the meaning of life. At the end of Ecclesiastes, he concluded with this: "Now all has been heard; here is the conclusion of the matter: Fear God and keep his commandments, for this is the whole duty of man" (Eccl. 12:13 ESV). If we are to become virtuous, we must set out to discover what, exactly, it means to fear the Lord. And we must in turn pass this timeless quality on to our daughters. The Bible mentions several types of fear, so we need to understand the type of fear spoken of in the phrase "fear of the Lord." At first glance, we might wonder if the fear of the Lord is the same type of fear we are most accustomed to experiencing, one best equated with being "afraid."

The *Holman Illustrated Bible Dictionary* describes secular fear as the natural feeling of alarm caused by the expectation of imminent danger, pain, or disaster while religious fear appears as the result of awe and reverence toward a supreme power. It goes on to say that this sense of fear comes as individuals encounter the divine in the context of revelation. When God appears to a person, the person experiences the reality of God's holiness. This self-disclosure of God points to the vast distinction between humans and God, to the mysterious characteristic of God that at the same time attracts and repels. A mystery in divine holiness causes individuals to become overwhelmed with a sense of awe and fear. It further concludes that the fear of God is not to be understood as the dread that comes out of fear of punishment, but as the reverential regard and the awe that comes out of recognition and submission to the divine. It is the revelation of God's will to which the believer submits in obedience.[2]

New Unger's Bible Dictionary describes fear of the Lord as something that:

- Dreads God's displeasure
- Desires God's favor
- Reveres God's holiness
- Submits cheerfully to God's will

- Is grateful for God's benefits
- Sincerely worships God
- Conscientiously obeys God's commandments[3]

It also states that fear and love must coexist in us before we can please and rightly serve God. Apparently God knew we would need to possess a godly fear before we could adequately grasp His heavenly love. The Proverbs 31 woman clearly had learned to fear the Lord and, as a result, served Him faithfully and wholeheartedly. No doubt, she had been set apart and Proverbs 31:29 records her legacy that "many women do noble things, but you surpass them all." It will be impossible for our daughters to live a life of purpose apart from developing a healthy "fear of the Lord." It is not surprising that fear of the Lord is the critical component that sets the virtuous woman apart from other women. A woman who fears the Lord has made the Lord the very foundation of her life.

The passage is just as meaningful today as it was when it was originally written. As we consider this recipe for raising virtuous daughters, it will be impossible to impart these truths to our girls unless we first own them for ourselves. While that may sound like a tall order, let's remember that we are each a work in progress. As Paul and Timothy reminded the saints in Philippi, "In all my prayers for all of you, I always pray with joy because of your partnership in the gospel from the first day until now, being confident of this, that he who began a good work in you will carry it on to completion until the day of Christ Jesus" (Phil. 1:4–6). Becoming a virtuous woman is a lifelong pursuit. The first step on the pathway of that pursuit begins when we take our eyes off ourselves and put them on Jesus.

Chapter 14

Grounded for Life

● ● ● ● ● ●

For while bodily training is of some value, godliness is
of value in every way, as it holds promise for the
present life and also for the life to come. (1 Tim. 4:8 ESV)

One of my greatest blessings in life is seeing my adult children
own their Christian faith. All three of my children (and
their spouses) love the Lord and are actively involved in their local
churches. In addition, they are raising their children to love the
Lord with their heart, soul, mind, and strength. When it comes to
passing down a legacy of faith to our children, parents today will
face many obstacles. One LifeWay study found that seven in ten
Protestants ages eighteen to thirty—both evangelical and mainline—who went to church regularly in high school said they quit
attending by age twenty-three. Among those, 34 percent had not
returned to church, even sporadically, by age thirty.[1] Another study
estimates the exodus as even higher claiming "90 percent of youth

active in high school church programs drop out of church by the time they are sophomores on college."[2] Why are so many of our children who are raised in the church, turning their back on the faith in their young adult years? One likely factor is that we are living in a post-Christian culture where it is no longer the norm to practice the Christian faith. In fact, America's Changing Religious Landscape Study (Pew Research Center) found that over a period of just seven years (2007–2014) "the percentage of Americans who are religiously unaffiliated—describing themselves as atheist, agnostic or 'nothing in particular'—has jumped more than six points, from 16.1 percent to 22.8 percent."[3]

Another factor that is no doubt contributing to the increase among young adults leaving the church is a failure among Christian parents to instill in their children a Christian worldview. In the book, *Soul Searching: The Religious and Spiritual Lives of American Teenagers*, authors Christian Smith and Melinda Lundquist found "the de facto dominant religion among contemporary U.S. teenagers is what they call 'Moralistic Therapeutic Deism': A God exists who created and orders the world and watches over human life on earth; God wants people to be good, nice, and fair to each other, as taught in the Bible and by most world religions; the central goal of life is to be happy and to feel good about oneself; God does not need to be particularly involved in one's life except when God is needed to resolve a problem; and good people go to heaven when they die." They add that a "majority of teenagers are incredibly inarticulate about their faith, religious beliefs and practices, and its place in their lives."[4] While this news is discouraging, my prayer is that it would be a wake-up call for Christian parents to be fully engaged in grounding their children for life in the Christian faith. In years past, a parent could assume that for the most part, their children would grow up in a culture that shared the same Christian values, but that is no longer the case. The tide has shifted and rather than stand on the banks and wring our hands as our children are swept downstream in a post-Christian tidal wave, parents need to rise up and take responsibility for the discipleship of their children.

While the news is certainly grim, I find myself feeling an undertone of excitement over the challenge that lies ahead. It will no longer be possible to coast along in our faith or rely on the local church as a spiritual filling station. Those of us who are wholeheartedly committed to living a life of purpose for the glory of God will have to double down on efforts and be intentional on passing the torch of faith to our children. We will need all hands on deck. Parents, grandparents, aunts, uncles, children's and youth pastors, teachers, coaches, neighbors, and anyone who has spiritual influence over this next generation will need to band together and point our children to the God we have so faithfully followed. But that's not all. We must make sure they understand the basic tenets of the Christian faith. As parents, we are called to be the primary disciplers of our children. Local churches, Christian private schools, and other Christian organizations can assist us in the task of discipleship, but ultimately it falls on our shoulders. God entrusted our children to our care in order that we raise them to be godly seed for the next generation. If we had to sum up our divinely assigned purpose as parents, it would be to raise children who love God with their hearts, souls, mind, and strength, put Christ at the center of their worship, and share Christ with a lost and dying world. It is not to raise children who live life as safely as possible and hop from pleasure to pleasure in a desperate attempt to fill the void in their hearts. It is not to raise children who make straight A's, excel in a sport, make the team, win awards, or earn college scholarships. It is not to raise children who someday excel in their careers and amass financial wealth. And believe it or not, it is not to raise children who are "happy," because happiness will not soothe the ache in their hearts for something more. That something is Jesus and it's up to us to make sure we not only tell them that, but show them with our own lives.

Study after study has shown that parents who are intentional when it comes to discipling their children are far more likely to raise solid, Christian children who grow up to be solid, Christian adults. One Barna study of Gen Z kids found that "kids whose parents are consciously, intentionally training their minds and hearts in the ways of Jerusalem are much better prepared."[5] The same Barna study concluded that Gen Z teens who fell into the category of "engaged Christians" were much more likely to hold beliefs that were consistent with the truths of the Bible. "Engaged Christians" readily identified as Christian and strongly agreed with the following: the Bible is the inspired Word of God and contains truth about the world. I have made a personal commitment to Jesus Christ that is still important in my life today. I engage with my church in more ways than just attending services. I believe that Jesus Christ was crucified and raised from the dead to conquer sin and death.[6] Additionally, four out of five engaged Christian teens agree "I can share my honest questions, struggles and doubts with my parents (79%), far more than any other faith segment.[7]

Sadly, when youth pastors in the same survey were given a list of thirteen common challenges they face in ministry, two-thirds (or 68%) say their biggest struggle is "parents not prioritizing their teen's spiritual growth."[8] This likely explains why the broader category of "churched teens" (as opposed to "engaged Christian teens) held beliefs and views about Christianity and the Bible that fell more in line with those of "unchurched teens." In a nutshell, parents who recognize that God has appointed them as the primary disciplers of their children are far more likely to take matters into their own hands when it comes to the spiritual training of their children rather than rely on the church to take up the task. A Sunday morning pep-talk by a Sunday school teacher or youth minister is not enough to equip your children to be "engaged Christians" the remaining six days of the week. Your investment in training your children to have a biblical worldview will have a direct impact on whether or not they choose to carry that faith with them in the future.

Grounded in God's Word

In the December 1948 *Ladies' Home Journal*, the following ad for Oxford Bibles can be found: "This Christmas . . . give your child the Bible. A fine Bible is the rightful inheritance of every young American. As the Pilgrims drew from it their dream that this nation might be founded in freedom . . . and Roosevelt his dream of the Four Freedoms for all the nations of the world . . . so from its pages today's young leaders will build tomorrow."[9] One of my most treasured possessions is a children's Bible my maternal grandparents gave me when I was ten years old. In my middle school and high school years, I remember retrieving the Bible off my bookshelf from time to time when I was experiencing a time of difficulty, confusion, or sadness. I would sit on my daybed, brush the dust off the cover and open the book, somehow knowing it contained the remedy for my distress. The Bible had a very basic concordance in the back that listed helpful verses to look up in times of need. I remember being particularly comforted by Psalm 23 and memorizing it. Strangely, I was comforted by this Shepherd spoken of in the psalm, though I had yet to formally meet Him. When it came time for me to go to college, I packed that children's Bible in my suitcase just in case I needed it. I was far from God's path at the time with little interest in God, yet I sensed it might come in handy. Coincidentally, my same grandparents who had given me that Bible years prior lived a short distance from the college I attended and would be a huge influence in my decision to follow Christ several years later at the age of twenty-one.

If our children are to build upon a firm foundation of faith, God's Word must be their treasured possession. It is our job to make sure they know the Bible is God's revelation to mankind, reliable, and relevant to today. In this digital age, many have traded their bulky leather Bibles for apps on their phones or tablets. One downside to this is that children do not witness their parents reading the Bible. Likewise, I feel it's important for our children to own an actual Bible from their earliest years. How else will they know the Bible is set apart as sacred and special if it's nothing more than just another app on their phone or tablet? Ephesians 6:17 reminds us to "take . . . the sword of the Spirit, which is the word of God." God has equipped our daughters with this "sword" to battle the culture. As mothers, it will be our responsibility to teach them to arm themselves for battle with the Word of God. Most of our youth today have been indoctrinated by the popular thinking of the day concerning a moral relativism which denies absolute standards of right and wrong behavior. In a culture that preaches moral relativism and political correctness, it is easy for even Christians to lose sight of the fact that absolute standards of right and wrong behavior are contained in God's Word. If we are to equip our daughters to stand against the moral relativism they will face, we must help them become convinced that the Bible is not a book, but is the accurate revelation of God and His standards to mankind. It is best if we can do so before seeds of doubt are planted in their minds by the culture.

The Bible contains God's words, truths, standards, and principles. It reveals His character and presents His message of love and redemption to all mankind. Paul reminds us in 2 Timothy 3:16 that "all Scripture is God-breathed." God inspired over forty authors to write the Bible over a span of 1,500 years. If our children fail to see the Bible as divinely inspired by God, it will become nothing more to them than just another good book containing simple suggestions brought by mere men. However, if they come to realize that God is, in fact, the Author of the Bible, they will much more easily understand and accept that the Bible is the final authority in all matters of life. The Bible trumps the popular opinions of the day brought by our culture. It changes everything. I made it a habit to tell my children that the Bible is God's love letter to each and every person. It reveals His heart to the people and unveils His eternal plan for all mankind.

It is not enough to teach our children to believe in Jesus because the "Bible says so." We must go a step further and teach them *why* we are confident the Bible was written by God through men. "The Bible says so" won't cut it as an effective argument in defending Christianity, matters of morality, or wooing someone to the Christian faith. It may have worked fifty years ago when most people accepted the Bible's divine origins without question. Today, the Bible is thought by many to be nothing more than a compilation of man-made opinions. It's not a matter of "if" our children will be challenged in regard to their beliefs concerning the origin of the Bible, but "when." If our daughters begin to doubt the reliability of the Bible, they will likely also begin to doubt the validity of the claims of Jesus, standards of right and wrong, and characteristics of

God that are recorded in the Bible. Such doubt will weaken the very foundation of their Christian faith.

There is an overwhelming amount of archaeological evidence to support the validity of the Bible. Prior to the nineteenth century there were many facts in historical accounts of the Bible that could not be confirmed. As a result, severe attacks concerning the legitimacy of the Bible were launched in the nineteenth century. It was claimed that people and places recorded in early Scripture were legend, not historical fact. Shortly after these attacks began, an explosion of archaeological finds took place. The existence of places and people described in the Old Testament was proved credible with the discoveries of ancient civilizations in Egypt, Babylonia, Palestine, and Assyria. The Bible continues to be historically verified by archaeology. It is exciting to think of the archeological finds that will occur in the years to come that will further support the validity of God's Word.

While most books have a short lifespan, the Bible has stood the test of time. To top it all off, the Bible is the best-selling book of all time. When you stop and think about the longevity of the Bible, it is nothing short of a miracle. In 1 Peter, we are reminded, "The grass withers and the flowers fall, but the word of the Lord stands forever" (1 Pet. 1:24b–25a). God's principles set forth in His Word are timeless for all ages. Our daughters need to know that God has left us the Bible as an instruction manual for living. J. I. Packer warns, "Disregard the study of God, and you sentence yourself to stumble and blunder through life blindfolded, as it were, with no sense of direction and no understanding of what surrounds you. This way you can waste your life and lose your soul."[10] God's standards, principles, and truths will act as a compass to steer them in the right direction (even when Mom is not there to help!) and give them the ability to filter right from wrong, good from evil, and wisdom from folly. Of course, in order for our daughters to partake in this wonderful treasure, they will need to recognize its value and come to depend on it as a source of sustenance in their daily lives.

Grounded in Prayer

Prayer, simply put, is conversing with God. The more our daughters converse with God, the more in touch they will be with His intended purpose for their lives. A consistent prayer life can act as a safeguard against mediocrity and a tendency toward a lukewarm Christian faith. Well-balanced "conversations" with God include both talking to God and listening to Him. After all, how good would a relationship with a friend be if our conversations always boiled down to a long to-do list for the other person. Philippians 4:6 says, "by prayer and petition, with thanksgiving, present your requests to God." There is certainly nothing wrong with asking God to do things for us, but there are other aspects of prayer that are also important. One of the simplest and best prayer models I have found that leads to a well-balanced prayer life is the ACTS model. ACTS is an acronym that stands for adoration (or praise), confession, thanksgiving, and supplication (making requests of God for others or ourselves). My husband and I taught the ACTS model to our children and utilized it as part of their bedtime ritual. We began teaching them this model of prayer when our youngest child was about four years old. By the time he was six, he could tell you what each letter stood for and give a basic definition of each word. We found the ACTS model to be very user-friendly for children of all ages.

At bedtime, my husband or I would start prayer time with our children by speaking words of adoration (praise) to God. We then allowed our child to do the same. We would go back and forth, taking turns on each aspect of ACTS. This way, it helped our kids understand what each aspect of ACTS meant and helped them put it into practice. Once they began to grasp praying the ACTS model, we had them pray it themselves. Prayer is a vital component of the Christian faith. When our children are taught to converse with God on a consistent basis, it personalizes the relationship and reminds them that God is present at all times.

A = *Adoration*

It seems only fitting that prayer to a Holy God should begin with acknowledgment to His divine characteristics and attributes. Our relationship with God is put into the proper perspective when we as the creation submit in awe and reverence to our Creator. It is an expression of faith when we take the focus off our own needs and direct our attention to the very One who promises to meet our needs. We adore God for His many attributes and just as we desire for someone to know and accept us for who we are, God desires the same from us. Scripture teaches us that God is loving, just, patient, long-suffering, everlasting, trustworthy, merciful, wise, holy, almighty, sovereign, omnipresent, forgiving, faithful, and the list goes on and on. The more we study God's Word, the more we get to know Him. (In the appendix, I have included a list of character qualities of God to use when praising Him.)

C = *Confession*

Confession is basically agreeing with God over our sin and feeling sorrow for our sin. Unless we think and feel the same way about our sin that God does, we will not repent of our sin (2 Cor. 7:10). When I would get to the confession part of prayer time with my children, I encouraged them to think of something specific that they had done or said that day, rather than make a general sweeping statement. (Ex: "Lord, I confess that I was wrong when I spoke disrespectfully to my mom when she picked me up late from school" vs. "Lord, I confess that sometimes I can be disrespectful to my parents.") If their confession involves a wrongdoing against another person, encourage them to make it right with the person by asking for forgiveness. Also, if you are taking turns going back and forth with the ACTS model, allow your daughter to hear you confess some specific sin that you committed that day. In doing so, we model to them that we (yes, even moms!) all have sinned and fall short of the glory of God (Rom. 3:23).

When our daughters confess their sins on a daily basis and acknowledge God's forgiveness, it reminds them that sin is a serious matter in the eyes of God. In a world that preaches moral relativism, the discipline of confession will remind our daughters that there are absolute moral standards that dictate right and wrong, and good and evil. However, we should be quick to assure our daughters that no sin is too big for the forgiveness of God. First John 1:9 promises that "If we confess our sins, [God] is faithful and just and will forgive us our sins and purify us from all unrighteousness." We must help our daughters recognize and respond properly to the pangs of conviction brought by the Holy Spirit over wrongdoing. We must equip them with the tools to acknowledge the conviction, confess their sins, and repent. If the habit of confession is developed early on in our daughters' lives, the chances increase that when they are older, they will rush to God's throne of grace in full confidence, knowing that they will receive His mercy and grace in their time of need (Heb. 4:16).

T = Thanksgiving

When I think of the need to thank God, I am reminded of the ten lepers spoken of in Luke 17:12–18. They all cried out to Jesus to have pity on them and heal them. He responded to their cries and told them to "Go, show yourselves to the priests," and then He healed them on their way. Unfortunately, only one bothered to return and thank Him. Jesus asked the man, "Were not all ten cleansed? Where are the other nine? Has no one returned to give praise to God except this foreigner?" (v. 17). Often, I am guilty, like the nine lepers, of failing to thank God for answered prayers. As hard as it is to remember to thank God when He answers our prayers, it is even harder to thank Him when He answers, but not in a way we had hoped. Nonetheless, in 1 Thessalonians 5:18, God calls us to "give thanks in all circumstances." This is the mark of true Christian maturity.

God reminds us in Psalm 50:23 that "those who sacrifices thank offerings honor me." In addition to teaching our daughters to thank God for answered prayer, we should also teach them to express thanks for things that they might otherwise take for granted. This would include the blessings of family, extended family, church family, a place to live, food to eat, freedom to worship, and the list goes on and on. Once again, if they hear us express thanks to God for our many blessings, we model what it looks like to have a heart of gratitude.

S = Supplication

Supplication is when we submit our requests or petitions to God on behalf of ourselves or others. As a reflection of the principle of putting others before ourselves, I encouraged my children to submit requests for others before praying for themselves. We can help them develop the habit of thinking of others first by gently asking them, "Is there anyone you would like to pray for tonight?" As they get older, they may want some privacy when they are praying for others or themselves. We should not take it personally, as our goal is to raise daughters who are comfortable conversing one on one with God. As your daughter begins to gain independence, you might say a quick prayer for her at bedtime and then leave her to pray alone. It is no different than other areas of training. The goal is to give our daughters a foundation for a healthy prayer life and assist them until they can master it on their own.

We must teach our daughters early on that God is the Father of compassion and the God of all comfort who is capable of comforting them in all their troubles (2 Cor. 1:3–4). "Troubles" can range from an "owie" when they're two, a parent's divorce when they are ten, failing to make the select team at thirteen, a breakup when they are seventeen, or anything, for that matter, that leads to tears or a broken heart. Girls who learn to run to Jesus in times of sadness or suffering are less likely to turn to other unhealthy things when seeking comfort. As much as we desire to protect our daughters from hurtful situations in life, it will be impossible. While it is a wonderful thing if our daughters count us as trusted confidants when they are hurting, we need to be careful to show them comfort, while at the same time, pointing them in the direction of the only One who can mend a broken heart.

Hebrews 5:7 says, "During the days of Jesus' life on earth, he offered up prayers and petitions with fervent cries and tears to the one who could save him from death, and he was heard because of his reverent submission." Because Jesus had submitted to His Father's authority even before His Father had answered His prayer, He was at peace regardless of the answer. Submission to God expressed through prayer says, "Your will be done," even if it is an answer they had not expected. If our daughters understand this concept, they will be less likely to question why God may choose not to answer some of their prayers in the ways they had hoped. They will understand that "no," or "wait," is as valid an answer to their prayers as "yes."

We must teach our daughters that God is accessible every minute of every day. When they develop the instinct to turn to God throughout their day, whether to lift up a request or a praise to Him, they will learn the art of what it is to pray without ceasing (1 Thess. 5:17). Children who develop the habit of taking thought of and talking to God throughout each day on their own initiative are much less likely to fall into tempting situations or make foolish decisions when standing at the crossroads of a difficult choice.

Grounded in Purpose

In Mark, chapter 12, Jesus was asked by one of the teachers of the law, "Of all the commandments, which is the most important?" (v. 28). Jesus answers, "The most important one," answered Jesus, "is this: 'Hear, O Israel, the Lord our God, the Lord is one. Love the Lord your God with all your heart and with all your soul and with all your mind and with all your strength.' The second is this: 'Love your neighbor as yourself.' There is no commandment greater than these" (Mark 12:29–31). In Jesus' answer, our purpose is found. The sum total of our lives is to love God and love others. And yet, we have made it so complicated. As parents, we knock ourselves out trying to provide our children with all the trappings that promise future happiness. We spend ungodly amounts of money on the latest and greatest toys and gadgets and yet, they are one of the unhappiest generations on record. We invest endless amounts of time shuttling them to a plethora of extracurricular activities in the hopes it will give them a sense of worth and value, and yet, there is an epidemic of mental health issues among their generation. When we think in terms of their future, we emphasize grades, academics, and college more than Bible study, prayer, and evangelism. Sadly, even if we provide them with all of the worldly trappings above, they will still lack purpose. God wired their hearts to long for something more—Him.

As evidence points to more and more churched teens abandoning a biblical worldview and trading it for a type of moralistic therapeutic deism that is steeped in personal happiness, we must be prepared to show our children why this will leave them empty in the end. That brand of non-faith won't rescue them from the consequences of sin and eternal separation from God. As I have said before, God has wired our hearts for His unfailing love and redemption. Nothing else will satisfy us in the end, including the futile pursuit of personal happiness. If we are faithful in exposing the lies associated with this faulty belief, we will raise daughters who are not only grounded in their faith, but also prepared to minister to their peers who come up empty and are left wanting for more. In Matthew 9:37–38, Jesus reminds us that the harvest is plentiful, but the laborers are few. He tells us to pray earnestly to the Lord of the harvest to send out laborers. Never before has it been more important to raise our children to walk in Truth and lead with love. Our task is not to simply raise children who are grounded in the faith, but to also rise up laborers who are prepared to share Jesus with an ever-increasing harvest of lost and empty souls.

Make no mistake. We are grounding our daughters in *something*. There is only one foundation worth building upon. There is only one foundation that will stand the test of time. There is only one foundation that will provide our daughters with the security their hearts long for. There is only one foundation that will carry them through this life and into the next. That foundation is Jesus Christ. All else is sinking sand. Is your daughter grounded for life?

Chapter Fifteen

The Heart of the Matter

● ● ● ● ● ●

*Whoever has the Son has life; whoever does not have
the Son of God does not have life. (1 John 5:12)*

In this final chapter I want to speak to you candidly about the challenge to raise godly daughters in an ungodly world. I want to come to you as a mother, not a writer with "expert opinions" (sorry, I'm not qualified!). Too often we pick up parenting books with the goal of finding some sort of tried and true formula for raising healthy and happy kids. You know, the kind of kids who grow up to say "please" and "thank-you," "yes ma'am" and "no sir." The kind who make their beds in the morning, share their toys with their siblings (without being told), and get gold stars on spelling tests.

Deep in our hearts we long to see evidence that we're on the right track with this parenting thing. In school and the workplace there are six-weeks grade reports and yearly employee evaluations to review progress and make any necessary changes along the way.

Not so with parenting, which is why we have a tendency to gravitate toward how-to books, depend on occasional pats on the back, or even translate our daughter's successes as our own personal successes. Our daughters are a reflection of us, and whether we want to admit it or not, we've all been guilty of trying to ensure that everything looks neat, tidy, and pretty on the outside. Some more so than others, but alas, we all lean in that direction. And let's face it, it's just plain easier to focus on the outside, where we can see evidences of positive change . . . and so can others.

The truth is we can train our daughters to be virtuous, polite, obedient, selfless, honest, and humble, but if their behavior is not motivated by a love for Christ and a desire to follow Him, they are relying on goodness rather than godliness. Isaiah 64:6 reminds us that our righteous acts are like filthy rags. But the sternest warning comes from Christ and His harsh words to the Pharisees: "Woe to you, teachers of the law and Pharisees, you hypocrites! You clean the outside of the cup and dish, but inside they are full of greed and self-indulgence. Blind Pharisee! First clean the inside of the cup and dish, and then the outside also will be clean" (Matt. 23:25–26).

Few would argue that many of our churches are filled with Pharisees who embrace a gospel of goodness over godliness. Admittedly there have been times when I've lapsed into that frame of mind. If we want to raise daughters who are not only "good girls," but more important, "godly girls," we must teach them to keep "the inside of the cup clean." In order to do that, we must not shy away from talking about sin and God's redemptive story. Sin is not merely a behavior but rather a condition. Fortunately, God provides a solution for our sin. It's our job to share the good news with our daughters.

Godliness Over Goodness

It's easy to focus on behavior modification strategies when it comes to training our daughters in godliness. I've been guilty at times of focusing more on changing my children's sinful behaviors than encouraging them to turn to the only One who can change their hearts and their sinful behavior. And while I could manipulate their behavior (at least at some level in the early years) in order to achieve a desired end result, I have no control when it comes to changing their hearts. Yet this is where true change must occur. Employing behavior modification strategies without addressing the heart does nothing more than put a Band-Aid on the problem. We must get to the heart of the matter.

Unless (or until) our children are believers in Christ, their motivation and ability to change sinful behaviors will be rooted solely on their own human willpower. Yet for believers, true change occurs when our hearts respond to conviction of sin with a godly sorrow rather than a worldly sorrow (2 Cor. 7:10) and, as a result, turn from the sin (repent). The motivation to change is the unfailing love of God in that "while we were still sinners, Christ died for us" (Rom. 5:8). His kindness leads us toward repentance (Rom. 2:4)—the kind of kindness the father exhibited to his son in the account of the prodigal son when he ran to him and greeted him with a hug and a kiss. No one and no thing can offer our children that brand of unfailing love.

It's easy to react to our daughters' sins with a set of swift consequences that discourage a repeat of the sins. However, we need to take the time to address the sins at the heart level in an effort to offer a permanent solution. We can't make our daughters experience godly sorrow or, for that matter, even repent, but we can remind them of their need for a Savior and the price that was paid. When my children were new drivers and would leave the house with car keys in hand to meet up with friends, I used to yell out a last-minute reminder to "make good choices!" When I think back on my habit of shouting out this reminder, I have to laugh. How many of our teens when faced with a tempting situation will stop, remember their mothers' sage advice, and declare to their friends, "Sorry guys, but my mom told me to 'make good choices,' so I'm going to have to pass"? It's wishful thinking on our parts, but not likely to happen. Even if it did work, the motivation would be misplaced. Modifying and managing behavior won't change your heart. My husband and I were forced to realize this with our youngest son who was not respondent to our familiar behavior modification parenting strategies. Only when we began to shift our attention to his heart rather than his behavior did we begin to see change. When he would leave the house with car keys in hand, I would yell out, "Remember the cross!" Reflecting on the sacrifice Christ made on the cross is far more likely to evoke a change in behavior than a parent pep talk to "make good choices."

One of the verses I often share when speaking at events is Psalm 26:2–3, "Test me, O LORD, and try me, examine my heart and my mind; for your love is ever before me, and I walk continually in your truth" (NIV, 1984). We must teach our daughters to lay their hearts bare before God on a regular and consistent basis. They are more likely to "walk continually in His truth" when they are in the habit of looking to God for an honest appraisal concerning the motives of their hearts. And of course, their motivation to stay on God's path is found in keeping His amazing, unfailing love ever before them.

Even Good Christian Kids Mess Up

Some months ago I received an e-mail from a mother who was distraught to learn that her daughter, whom she described as a "good, Christian girl" had had sex. Her daughter was a junior in college and dating a "good, Christian guy" who was in his first year of seminary. Her daughter was living at home, and the mother stumbled upon a note from GCG (good, Christian guy) that indicated they had had sex. She was devastated that this "future pastor in training had as she described, "robbed her daughter of her virginity." Her purpose for writing me was to ask if she should come clean and tell her daughter about finding the note and encourage her to break up with GCG. She included excerpts from the note as evidence that they had clearly had sex. And based on her report, it was clear her daughter was a willing party.

Strangely, when I read it, I walked away with a completely different impression of GCG. I was most struck by the sincere regret he expressed in the note that they had "slipped up." His purpose for writing was to let her know he had experienced tremendous conviction and, after spending time in prayer over their sin, had felt led to take steps "to guard and protect her heart in the future." Some of the steps he listed included weekly accountability to an older, godly man, not spending time alone together in their apartments when their roommates were gone, and spending some time reading God's Word together and praying. But what really struck me was the godly sorrow he expressed in the note over what had happened and, more important, his desire to get back on track in his relationship with God, both for his sake and for his girlfriend's sake.

So in a nutshell, there was a sin (a wrong turn at the crossroads); there was conviction over the sin, ownership of the sin (on the boyfriend's part), and godly sorrow that followed; there was an immediate U-turn and new direction; and there was a plan in place (as a result of his initiative) to hold him further accountable in the future in order that he might "protect and guard her heart." And this mother wants her daughter to break up with this guy? Through her hurt and disappointment over the loss of her daughter's virginity (by her daughter's own choice), this mother had failed to see that even though this good, Christian guy did a not-so-good thing, he chose to respond in a good and, more important, *godly* manner. In fact, he was the one who responded to conviction over the sin and initiated an accountability plan! Perhaps, her worries were misplaced, since from what I could tell, her daughter was experiencing little if any, guilt and conviction.

Sometimes good Christian guys and good Christian girls do, in fact, make not-so-good choices. I know some of you mothers with younger children may not want to hear that good Christian kids do, in fact, sin because, like me, maybe you imagined that if you did all the right things (read the latest and greatest parenting book; take them to church every Sunday; raise them on VeggieTales; sign them up for VBS every summer; involve them in youth group at church; send them to Christian camps and events; sign them up for mission trips; etc.) that somehow you can protect them from making some of the same foolish choices you may have made. Sorry to be the one to burst your bubble. Those are all wonderful things; and, no doubt, you are making "holy deposits" along the way. However, your daughters will not be exempt from saying yes to temptations and straying from God's path. I know this because I was once you. And when my children strayed, I would somehow manage to blame *myself*.

In spite of our best efforts, our daughters (yes, even the good Christian ones) are going to sin at times. Just as we do. Part of being a good parent is to teach our children how to get back up when they fall down. Not pretend they never will or, even worse, pick them up and give them a quick brush-off before the neighbors see them. It's far more difficult to raise a *godly girl* than a *good girl*. And if we're honest, we also know it's far more difficult to be a *godly mom* than a *good mom*.

Final Thoughts

When I became a Christian at the age of twenty-one, I was a mess of a girl with a sin list a mile long. I was your typical girl who bought the lies of the culture and suffered plenty of fallout along the way. No doubt, it would have taken several U-haul trucks to haul my sins to the foot of the cross, but fortunately Jesus did the dirty work for me. God, in His mercy, had forgiven my sins, and behold, I became a new creation (see 2 Cor. 5:17).

In the days that followed my conversion to Christianity, I felt like a wrecking ball had been released and the flimsy structure my life had previously been built on came crumbling to the ground in a pile of dusty ashes and debris. God took one look at my old life and deemed it uninhabitable. With the care of a master architect, He laid a new foundation and the rebuilding process began. In truth, it would take nearly a decade to repair the damage sustained from twenty-one years of believing the lies. One board, one nail, one brick at a time, God helped me replace each lie with His amazing truth.

Two years after becoming a Christian (which marked the demolition of my old life), I had my first child (a son) and within four years, I had my second (a daughter). My third child (a son) followed a couple of years later. I share that detail to say that my life was still very much in the rebuilding phase during my children's most impressionable years. You can't raze a structure and rebuild in a day, so needless to say, my early parenting years were when my own heart was under construction. And at the time, the thought certainly crossed my mind: How can I raise a daughter who resists the lies of the culture and builds a foundation on God's truths when I am still teetering on wobbly scaffolding, caulking the cracks of my own life? Of course, there was only one way. I would need God's help.

If you are feeling overwhelmed and grossly under-qualified with the task at hand, I want to encourage you. God can work His good in any situation if given the opportunity and I am living proof of that promise. The mother I am now to my daughter is not the mother I was when she was two, five, ten, or fourteen. And the person I am today, though much improved, is still desperately dependent on the Lord to take up the slack for my shortcomings. I don't know where you are in the parenting journey, but I want to remind you to be easy on yourself. None of us has it all together—even those of us writing the parenting books! You will make mistakes along the way. I know I did. You will second-guess decisions you have made. I know I did. It is a mother's tendency to wonder if you're doing enough. When that happens, remind yourself that God is sufficient. As much as you love your daughter and want to see her fall madly in love with Jesus and live a life devoted to Him, God loves her all the more and wants the same things for her.

When I penned my final thoughts on the original version of this book back in 2008, the timing was strangely ironic. It coincided with my daughter's graduation from high school. Needless to say, I wrote the book with a certain sense of urgency as the clock ticked louder and louder in the background of my own parenting journey, signaling the close of one chapter and the beginning of another.

As I mentioned in the introduction, it has been an interesting experience to update this book in the aftermath of my daughter's transition into adulthood. It's been ten years since I wrote the original version of this book and ironically, my daughter is now a mother of a daughter with many of the same worries and concerns that I once had. If I could leave you with a final word of encouragement, it would be this: Your diligence and persistence in raising your daughters to be godly young women will be worth it. However, the end goal in having these necessary conversations with your daughters should not be to raise perfectly well-behaved daughters who never slip-up or deviate from God's path. Good luck with that one! Sometimes, the most valuable lessons are lessons learned the hard way, by way of personal experience. It was hard to witness at the time, but now that I'm able to look back on my parenting journey, I see God's hand in every detail. I recognize the value of missteps along the way and how it's contributed to the godly young woman she is today.

I said before and I still believe it, "there is no foolproof formula when it comes to raising our children." I can't make any guarantees that reading this book and implementing the principles herein will produce the end result of a daughter who embraces God's truths and rejects the culture's lies. But I can tell you this: If you practice the principles contained on these pages and lean on the Lord for wisdom, strength, and discernment, you will have provided your daughter with the tools to embrace God's truths and reject the culture's lies. You can't force her to build her life on God's truths—she will have to make that decision on her own. At the end of the day, you don't answer to anyone but God. He has trusted you with the stewardship of your children while they were in your nest, and your call is to honor Him in the task and raise them, in turn, to bring honor to Him. You are not responsible for the results.

God is not looking for perfect mothers to raise perfect daughters. He's looking for imperfect mothers who are raising imperfect daughters in an imperfect world, and desperately dependent on a perfect God for the results.

Talk about It

Chapter 13

When reading the verses about the virtuous woman in the Proverbs 31 passage, which of her character qualities do you struggle with the most?

What about your daughter?

Do you feel this passage is still relevant for today when it comes to raising our daughters to be virtuous? Why or why not?

In looking over the definition of what it means to "fear the Lord," what changes might you need to make to be more virtuous?

How can you raise your daughter to fear the Lord?

Chapter 14

In what ways have you been intentional when it comes to training your daughter to embrace a biblical worldview?

Does your daughter view the Bible as the inerrant Word of God and her instruction manual for life?

Do you make it a regular habit to pray with your daughter? How comfortable is your daughter praying?

Chapter 15

Is it your tendency to emphasize godliness or goodness when parenting your daughter?

How might you emphasize heart examination over behavior modification?

Have you taught your daughter how to get back up when falling down (as a result of sin)?

Is it hard for you to trust God for the results when it comes to raising your daughter or do you feel responsible for the outcome?

Appendix

• • • • • •

Conversation 1

• • • • • • • • • • • • •

Beauty by the Book

Psalm 139:14	I praise you because I am fearfully and wonderfully made; your works are wonderful, I know that full well.

What it means: You are created in the image of God, and God doesn't make junk! Like a snowflake, every person is unique. No two are the same. God sees you as a masterpiece; and when you look in the mirror, He wants you to "know that full well." Try this beauty tip: Every morning when you look in the mirror, say Psalm 139:14 and smile. You might even tape the verse on your mirror as a reminder!

1 Samuel 16:7	But the LORD said to Samuel, "Do not consider his appearance or his height, for I have rejected him. The LORD does not look at the things man looks at. Man looks at the outward appearance, but the LORD looks at the heart."

What it means: The world focuses on what people look like on the outside. God focuses on what people look like on the inside. Do you put more time and effort into being pretty on the outside or the inside? As you get older, you will meet Christian girls who spend more time trying to find the perfect outfit, get the perfect tan, find the perfect lip gloss, and have the perfect body. While there's nothing wrong with wanting to look pretty, we need to make sure it's in balance. God would rather see us work on becoming drop-dead gorgeous on the inside. You know, the kind of girl who talks to Him on a regular basis (prayer) and reads her Bible.

Proverbs 31:30	Charm is deceptive, and beauty is fleeting; but a woman who fears the LORD is to be praised.

What it means: Beauty fades with age, so if you are more concerned with your outer appearance, you will be unhappy when the wrinkles come and the number on the scale goes up. In fact, did you know that your body may show the beginning signs of aging as early as age twenty? That is why God wants us to "fear" Him. That doesn't mean to be afraid of Him but rather to be in awe of Him and all that He has done. Let me put it to you this way. If you stand two girls next to each other and one is Miss Teen USA whose beauty is limited to physical beauty, and the other young lady is a more average-looking girl who loves the Lord more than anything, she is the more beautiful girl in the eyes of God.

1 Peter 3:3–4	Your beauty should not come from outward adornment, such as braided hair and the wearing of gold jewelry and fine clothes. Instead, it should be that of your inner self, the unfading beauty of a gentle and quiet spirit, which is of great worth in God's sight.

What it means: This does not mean it's wrong to braid your hair or wear nice clothes and jewelry. The verse was written to warn women not to follow the customs of some of the Egyptian women who, during that time period, spent hours and hours working on their hair, makeup, and finding the perfect outfit. God would rather see women work on becoming beautiful on the inside—the kind of beauty that lasts forever.

1 Timothy 4:8 NLT	Physical exercise has some value, but spiritual exercise is much more important, for it promises a reward in both this life and the next.

What it means: Exercising and staying in shape is a good thing, but God expects us to stay in shape spiritually by reading our Bibles, praying, and going to church on a regular basis. In other words, there will be plenty of people who put their time and effort into staying in shape but who are out of shape spiritually. If they don't know Jesus Christ, their perfect bodies won't get them through the gates of heaven.

If Your Daughter Is Five Years or Less

I would be willing to bet that most compliments paid to infants and toddlers are in regard to appearance. Of course, this is understandable considering we can't really highlight an infant's sparkling personality or good deeds accomplished. Chances are we heard,

"What a beautiful baby," on numerous occasions when our daughters were just infants. And chances are, we have said it countless times to others. While our infants are unable to absorb the message, it won't be long before they do. My daughter was often complimented as a baby for her blonde curls, blue eyes, fair skin, and teeny-tiny frame. She hardly looked old enough to walk when she took her first steps, and many claimed she looked like a little porcelain china doll. And trust me, by the age of two, she had taken note of each and every compliment.

I recall a day when she was just 2½ years old and we were walking by a shop window. She caught her reflection and said, "Oooohhhh, pwiddy gull." I laughed at the time, noting her confidence and wondering if it would bleed over into her teen years when she needed it most. The appearance-based compliments (from others and myself) continued through her toddler years. Until an occasion when she was four years old, I didn't realize there might be a downside to the praises. It was picture day at her preschool and I had dressed her up in a beautiful dress with a matching hair ribbon that held back her sweeping long blonde curls. As she was walking into the door of the classroom that morning, her teacher said, "Paige, you look so pretty!" Paige's response without even missing a beat was, "I know. Everyone tells me that."

Yikes! Of course, this was long before I was writing about the dangers of misdefined worth (more about that in chapter 3), not to mention I was hardly qualified since I was clearly part of the problem. From that day forward, I tried to emphasize her character qualities and de-emphasize her physical beauty. If she grew dependent on the compliments, what would become of her self-esteem when she entered the gawky, adolescent phase? You remember it, don't you? Pimples, bad hair days, and a body that often seemed out of control—truth be told, many of us are still in recovery from those days!

We must be careful to find a healthy balance when it comes to complimenting our child's appearance, especially in the early years. On the one hand, our girls naturally want to be told they are pretty. If we don't tell them, it could leave them craving male attention in the years to come. On the other hand, we don't want to go overboard and send a message that worth is based on what they look like. This, in turn, could set them up for disappointment when the compliments diminish over the years.

If Your Daughter Is Six to Eleven Years

As your daughter moves through grade school, she will begin to absorb the culture's message regarding beauty. Whether she is being influenced primarily by the media or her friends, one thing is for certain: she is hearing a buzz about what constitutes beauty in the world's eyes. It will be especially important in these years to have open communication with your daughter regarding these messages. Take advantage of teachable moments, whether they are ads you come across or a comment made by a friend. Remind her of 1 Samuel 16:17 and how God looks at the heart while the world looks at appearance. Continue to remind her of this passage as she moves through grade school. If she struggles with weight, emphasize a healthy diet and exercise and make sure you are practicing it yourself. Rather than nag her about eating too many sweets or snacks, try to reduce the temptation by minimizing them in your home. Lead by example. Whatever you do, never shame her about weight, even jokingly.

If your daughter seems to be overly attentive in these years to appearance and body image issues, you might want to look closely at her immediate circle to see where the influence is coming from. Is it a friend? Is she exposed to messages in the media that she is too young to process? (For example, is she allowed to engage in social media, watch shows on TV, or listen to music that supports a narrow and unrealistic definition of beauty?) Could you or your husband be focusing too much on appearance and sending her the wrong message? If you see warning signs, do what you can to reverse the damage, even if it means seeing a counselor or nutritionist. Many eating disorders take root in these years and, if not addressed, will only get worse.

Again, emphasize virtue and character qualities over appearance. This doesn't mean you go overboard and tell her appearance doesn't matter. The message should always be temple maintenance: healthy weight range, good eating habits, exercise, positive grooming habits. Because girls are developing earlier, your daughter will be exposed to many shapes and sizes during these years. It's important that you don't make comments about other girls (or your daughter) in these years that could leave them feeling inferior or worried about their own development process. As they move into the latter years of grammar school, begin necessary conversations with them about the process their body (and their friends' bodies) will go through as they move from girlhood to womanhood.

If Your Daughter Is Twelve Years or Older

When I surveyed adult Christian women, one of the questions I asked them was: "What sort of message did you receive from your mom and/or dad regarding weight/body image when you were growing up?" Many women shared that even today they could still remember exact phrases and the sting they felt over comments made by their parents during their middle and high school years.

"Are you sure you want seconds?"

"Have you checked the calorie count in that cookie?"

"You might want to lay off the _____."

"You're never going to get a husband if you keep eating like that."

Comments such as the ones above, made even in jest, will have an impact on our daughters. Even if your daughter needs to lose weight, it's best if the pediatrician breaks the news rather than her hearing it in the form of constant nagging by a parent. And for the record, if the pediatrician isn't worried, you shouldn't be either. Again, a better approach would be to emphasize nutrition and exercise and lead by example. Practice it; don't preach it.

For most of our daughters, the change in body shape will be most drastic in the span of years from twelve to eighteen. Most girls will have their womanly shape by the time they graduate high school. Many girls are caught off guard in these years when their bodies transition (almost overnight, it seems) from girlhood to womanhood. We must make sure they know that this is normal and part of God's design to prepare them someday to bear children (if that is part of God's plan).

If your daughter is in the twelve to eighteen age range, make sure your comments related to appearance, weight, and body shape of your daughter (and others) are scarce. If you are preoccupied with these things, chances are, your daughter will be as well. Allow your daughter to hear you compliment women who are truly worthy of being labeled beautiful—those who are virtuous. Most importantly, keep the conversation going over the years and remind her often, "You are more than the sum of your parts."

Conversation 2

• • • • • • • • • • • • • •

Signs Your Child Might Be Addicted

Early research on screen addiction has found that the amount of time spent on media consumption is not the biggest determinant of addiction, but rather, if it "causes problems in other areas of life or has become an all-consuming activity."[1]

Based on a key study related to technology and addiction among children, here are some warning signs that could indicate your child's media consumption has lapsed into a compulsive addiction:[2]

Unsuccessful Control: It is hard for my child to stop using screen media.

Loss of Interest: Screen media is the only thing that seems to motivate my child.

Preoccupation: Screen media is all my child seems to think about.

Psychosocial Consequences: My child's screen media use interferes with family activities.

Serious Problems Due to Use: My child's screen media use causes problems for the family.

Withdrawal: My child becomes frustrated when he/she cannot use screen media.

Tolerance: The amount of time my child wants to use screen media keeps increasing.

Deception: My child sneaks using screen media.

Escape/Relieve Mood: When my child has had a bad day, screen media seems to be the only thing that helps him/her feel better.

Monitoring Software Recommendations

(Note that oftentimes the technology changes and new and better software is introduced, so I encourage you to research the possibilities by googling "monitoring software mobile devices.")

http://www.toptenreviews.com/software/privacy/best-cell-phone-parental-control-software/

http://money.cnn.com/2014/09/03/technology/social/spy-on-snapchat/

https://meetcircle.com

Conversation 3

• • • • • • • • • • • • • •

STD Fact Sheet[3]

What are sexually transmitted diseases (STDs)?

STDs are diseases that are passed from one person to another through sexual contact. These include chlamydia, gonorrhea, genital herpes, human papillomavirus (HPV), syphilis, and HIV. Many of these STDs do not show symptoms for a long time. Even without symptoms, they can still be harmful and passed on during sex.

How are STDs spread?

You can get an STD by having vaginal, anal or oral sex with someone who has an STD. Anyone who is sexually active can get an STD. You don't even have to "go all the way" (have anal or vaginal sex) to get an STD. This is because some STDs, like herpes and HPV, are spread by skin-to-skin contact.

How common are STDs?

STDs are common, especially among young people. There are about 20 million new cases of STDs each year in the United States. About half of these infections are in people between the ages of fifteen and twenty-four.

Young people are at greater risk of getting an STD for several reasons:

- Young women's bodies are biologically more prone to STDs.

- Some young people do not get the recommended STD tests.
- Many young people are hesitant to talk openly and honestly with a doctor or nurse about their sex lives.
- Not having insurance or transportation can make it more difficult for young people to access STD testing.
- Some young people have more than one sex partner

What can I do to protect myself?

- The surest way to protect yourself against STDs is to not have sex. That means not having any vaginal, anal, or oral sex ("abstinence"). There are many things to consider before having sex. It's okay to say "no" if you don't want to have sex.
- If you do decide to have sex, you and your partner should get tested for STDs beforehand. Make sure that you and your partner use a condom from start to finish every time you have oral, anal, or vaginal sex. Know where to get condoms and how to use them correctly. It is not safe to stop using condoms unless you've both been tested for STDs, know your results, and are in a mutually monogamous relationship.
- Mutual monogamy means that you and your partner both agree to only have sexual contact with each other. This can help protect against STDs, as long as you've both been tested and know you're STD-free.
- Before you have sex, talk with your partner about how you will prevent STDs and pregnancy. If you think you're ready to have sex, you need to be ready to protect your body. You should also talk to your partner ahead of time

about what you will and will not do sexually. Your partner should always respect your right to say no to anything that doesn't feel right.

* Make sure you get the health care you need. Ask a doctor or nurse about STD testing and about vaccines against HPV and hepatitis B.

* Girls and young women may have extra needs to protect their reproductive health. Talk to your doctor or nurse about regular cervical cancer screening, and chlamydia and gonorrhea testing. You may also want to discuss unintended pregnancy and birth control.

* Avoid mixing alcohol and/or recreational drugs with sex. If you use alcohol and drugs, you are more likely to take risks, like not using a condom or having sex with someone you normally wouldn't have sex with.

If I get an STD, how will I know?

Many STDs don't cause any symptoms that you would notice. The only way to know for sure if you have an STD is to get tested. You can get an STD from having sex with someone who has no symptoms. Just like you, that person might not even know he or she has an STD.

Where can I get tested?

There are places that offer teen-friendly, confidential, and free STD tests. This means that no one has to find out you've been tested. Visit gettested.cdc.gov to find an STD testing location near you.

Can STDs be treated?

Your doctor can prescribe medicine to cure some STDs, like chlamydia and gonorrhea. Other STDs, like herpes, can't be cured, but you can take medicine to help with the symptoms. If you are ever treated for an STD, be sure to finish all of your medicine, even if you feel better before you finish it all. Ask the doctor or nurse about testing and treatment for your partner, too. You and your partner should avoid having sex until you've both been treated. Otherwise, you may continue to pass the STD back and forth. It is possible to get an STD again (after you've been treated), if you have sex with someone who has an STD.

What happens if I don't treat an STD?

Some curable STDs can be dangerous if they aren't treated. For example, if left untreated, chlamydia and gonorrhea can make it difficult—or even impossible—for a woman to get pregnant. You also increase your chances of getting HIV if you have an untreated STD. Some STDs, like HIV, can be fatal if left untreated.

What if my partner or I have an incurable STD?

Some STDs, like herpes and HIV, aren't curable, but a doctor can prescribe medicine to treat the symptoms.

If you are living with an STD, it's important to tell your partner before you have sex. Although it may be uncomfortable to talk about your STD, open and honest conversation can help your partner make informed decisions to protect his or her health.

If I have questions, who can answer them?

If you have questions, talk to a parent or other trusted adult. Don't be afraid to be open and honest with them about your concerns. If you're ever confused or need advice, they're the first place to start. After all, they were young once, too.

Talking about sex with a parent or another adult doesn't need to be a one-time conversation. It's best to leave the door open for conversations in the future.

It's also important to talk honestly with a doctor or nurse. Ask which STD tests and vaccines they recommend for you.

Teen Pregnancy Fact Sheet[4]

Almost 1,700 teenage girls get pregnant every single day. That's 70 girls every hour.[5]

Roughly 82 percent of teenage pregnancies aren't planned.[6]

Only 38 percent of teen mothers who have a child before they turn eighteen have a high school diploma, and less than 2 percent earn a college degree by age thirty.[7]

In 2014, one in six (17%) teen births to fifteen- to nineteen-year-olds were to girls who already had one or more babies.[8]

When you have sex for the first time determines your pregnancy risk: 46 percent of teenage girls and 22 percent of teenage boys who have sex *before* the age of fifteen have been involved in a pregnancy. For teens who have sex for the first time at fifteen or older, the risk declines to 25 percent and 9 percent, respectively.[9]

Thirty percent of teenage girls who drop out of high school do so because of pregnancy or parenthood.[10]

Two-thirds of young unmarried mothers are poor, with 25 percent going on welfare within three years of a child's birth.[11]

Even though teen pregnancy rates are at an all-time low, three in ten American teen girls still experience pregnancy.[12]

Compared to the teenage birth rates in other developed countries, America's are the highest: twice as high as Australia's and Canada's, three times as high as France's, three and a half times as high as Germany's, six times as high as the Netherlands', and seven times as high as Japan's.[13]

Only 20 percent of fathers of children born to teen moms marry the mothers.[14]

Roughly 18 percent of women having abortions in the U.S. are teens.[15]

Sexting Fact Sheet[16]

Start the Discussion Early

Start the conversation with your child by asking broad questions such as, "Have you heard of sexting? Tell me what you think it is." You can then frame your conversation around how much your child does or does not know. Seeing a story in the news, community, or at your child's school is a good prompt to check in again. Emphasize the consequences of sexting as shown by situations in the news where it has gone badly.

Use Examples Appropriate for Your Child's Age

For tweens with cell phones, let them know that text messages should never include images of anyone without clothes. For teenagers, be specific about what sexting is and that it can lead to serious consequences. For all ages, remind them that once an image is sent, it is no longer in their control and they cannot get it back. What is online or sent via text can exist forever and be sent to others.

Remind Your Teenager of Their Own Worth

Let your child know that being pressured to send a sext is not okay, nor is it a way to "prove" their love or show attraction. Let your child know you understand it is hard to be pressured or dared to do something but that they have the power to stand up for themselves. Remind your teenager that they are worthy of respect.

Sexual Assault Fact Sheet[17]

Sexual assault is any type of sexual activity or contact that you do not consent to.

Sexual assault can happen through physical force or threats of force or if the attacker gave the victim drugs or alcohol as part of the assault. Sexual assault includes rape and sexual coercion. In the United States, one in three women has experienced some type of sexual violence. If you have been sexually assaulted, it is not your fault, regardless of the circumstances.

What is sexual assault?

Sexual assault is any type of sexual activity or contact, including rape, that happens without your consent. Sexual assault can include non-contact activities, such as someone "flashing" you (exposing themselves to you) or forcing you to look at sexual images.

Sexual assault is also called sexual violence or abuse. Legal definitions of sexual assault and other crimes of sexual violence can vary slightly from state to state. If you've been assaulted, it is never your fault.

What does sexual assault include?

- Any type of sexual contact with someone who **cannot** consent, such as someone who is underage (as defined by state laws), has an intellectual disability, or is passed out (such as from drugs or alcohol) or unable to respond (such as from sleeping)
- Any type of sexual contact with someone who **does not** consent
- Rape
- Attempted rape
- Sexual coercion
- Sexual contact with a child
- Fondling or unwanted touching above or under clothes

Sexual assault can also be verbal, visual, or noncontact. It is anything that forces a person to join in unwanted sexual activities or attention. Other examples can include:

- Voyeurism, or peeping (when someone watches private sexual acts without consent)
- Exhibitionism (when someone exposes himself or herself in public)
- Sexual harassment or threats
- Forcing someone to pose for sexual pictures

- Sending someone unwanted texts or "sexts" (texting sexual photos or messages)

What does "consent" mean?

Consent is a clear "yes" to sexual activity. Not saying "no" does not mean you have given consent. Sexual contact without consent is sexual assault or rape.

Your consent means:

- You know and understand what is going on (you are not unconscious, blacked out, asleep, underage, or have an intellectual disability).
- You know what you want to do.
- You are able to say what you want to do or don't want to do.
- You are aware that you are giving consent (and are not impaired by alcohol or drugs).

Sometimes you cannot give legal consent to sexual activity or contact—for example, if you are:

- Threatened, forced, coerced, or manipulated into agreeing
- Not physically able to (you are drunk, high, drugged, passed out, or asleep)
- Not mentally able to (due to illness or disability)
- Under the age of legal consent, which varies by state (link is external)

Remember:

- **Consent is an ongoing process,** not a one-time question. If you consent to sexual activity, you can change your mind and choose to stop at any time, even after sexual activity has started.

- **Past consent does not mean future consent.** Giving consent in the *past* to sexual activity does not mean your past consent applies *now* or in the *future*.
- **Saying "yes" to a sexual activity is not consent for all types of sexual activity.** If you consent to sexual activity, it is only for types of sexual activities that you are comfortable with at that time with that partner. For example, giving consent for kissing does not mean you are giving consent for someone to remove your clothes.

What is NOT considered consent in sexual activity?

- **Silence.** Just because someone does not say "no" doesn't mean she is saying "yes."
- **Having consented before.** Just because someone said "yes" in the past does not mean she is saying "yes" now. Consent must be part of every sexual activity, every time.
- **Being in a relationship.** Being married, dating, or having sexual contact with someone before does not mean that there is consent now.
- **Being drunk or high.** Read more about alcohol, drugs, and sexual assault.
- **Not fighting back.** Not putting up a physical fight does not mean that there is consent.
- **Sexy clothing, dancing, or flirting.** What a woman or girl wears or how she behaves does not show consent for sexual activity. Only a verbal "yes" means "yes" to sexual activity.

Who commits sexual assault?

Sexual assault is most often committed by someone the victim knows. This may be a friend, an acquaintance, an ex, a relative, a date, or a partner. Less often, a stranger commits sexual assault. Women and men commit sexual assault, but more than 90 percent of people who commit sexual violence against women are men.

What is the average age a woman is sexually assaulted?

Four of every five women who are raped are raped before age twenty-five. About 40 percent of women who have been raped, or two in every five, were assaulted before age eighteen.

Conversation 5

• • • • • • • • • • • • •

Chapter 14: Characteristics of God (for ACTS prayer model)

Father/personal God

Love—unlimited and unconditional

Grace

Mercy

Holy

Righteous/perfect

Hates sin and unrighteousness (but loves sinners)

Just

Omniscient (all knowing)

All wise

Omnipotent (all powerful)

Sovereign

Omnipresent (everywhere at the same time)

Immutable (does not change)

Eternal (no beginning and no ending)

Infinite (not constrained by time or space)

Creator

Sustainer

Comforter

Patient

Faithful

Is Truth

Compassionate

Protector

Provider

Notes

● ● ● ● ● ●

Chapter 1: More Than the Sum of Your Parts

1. Anastasia Goodstein, "What Can Industry Do to Stop the Onslaught?" *The Huffington Post*, October 2, 2007, https://www.huffpost.com/entry/what-can-industry-do-to-s_b_66798.

2. Ibid.

3. The Dove Foundation, www.campaignforrealbeauty.com/press.asp?section=news&id=110.

4. Joan Jacobs Brumberg, *The Body Project: An Intimate History of American Girls* (New York: Random House, 1998), xxi.

5. Ibid., xx.

6. Ibid., 70.

7. Ibid., 107, picture 25.

8. Ibid., xxiv.

9. https://en.wikipedia.org/wiki/Female_body_shape; A study of the shapes of more than 6,000 women, carried out by researchers at the North Carolina State University circa 2005, for apparel, found that 46 percent were rectangular, just over 20 percent spoon, just under 14 percent inverted triangle, and 8 percent hourglass. Helen McCormack, "The Shape of Things to Wear: Scientists Identify How Women's Figures Have Changed in 50 Years," *The Independent*, (21 November 2005).

10. Ashley Marcin, "What's the Average Height for Women and How Does That Affect Weight?" https://www.healthline.com/health/womens-health/average-height-for-women; Medically reviewed by Janna Young, MPHon August 23, 2017.

11. https://en.wikipedia.org/wiki/Female_body_shape

12. Brumberg, *The Body Project*, 110.

13. https://www.commonsensemedia.org/children-teens-body-image-media-infographic

14. Lisa Berzins, "Dying to be thin: the prevention of eating disorders and the role of federal policy. APA co-sponsored congressional briefing," USA. November 1997.

15. Children, Teens, Media, and Body Image: A Common Sense Research Brief, January 21, 2015, https://www.commonsensemedia.org/research/children-teens-media-and-body-image.

16. August 8, 2017; https://adolescentgrowth.com/eating-disorder-statistics/.

17. Childhood Obesity Facts; https://www.cdc.gov/healthyschools/obesity/facts.htm.

18. U.S. Department for Health and Human Services, "Children and Teens Told by Doctors that They Were Overweight—United States, 1999–2002," Morbidity & Mortality Weekly Report 54, no. 34 (September 2, 2005): 848–49.

19. Ginny Olson, *Teenage Girls: Exploring Issues Adolescent Girls Face and Strategies to Help Them* (Grand Rapids, MI: Zondervan, 2006), 55–56.

20. J. A. O'Dea and S. Abraham, "Association Between Self-Concept and Body Weight, Gender, and Pubertal Development Among Male and Female Adolescents," *Adolescence* 34 (Spring 1999): 69–79.

21. Sarah Baicker, "For teens, obesity no laughing matter," October 23, 2007. According to new research from the University of Minnesota; Dianne Neumark-Sztainer, the study's lead researcher, tracked 2,500 adolescents over five years, news.medill.northwestern.edu/washington/news.aspx?id=66261.

22. Ibid.

23. Naomi Wolf, *The Beauty Myth: How Images of Beauty Are Used Against Women* (New York: Harper Perennial, 2002). Note: Although I disagree with the author's radical feminist views and negative view of Christianity, I found some of the research to be useful in citing the media's damage when it comes to the "beauty myth."

24. "Effects of Aging on Your Body," www.cnn.com/2007 /HEALTH/07/27/life.stages/index.html, accessed August 14, 2007.

25. Korin Miller, "Sad Proof That Most Women Don't Think They're Beautiful," April 7, 2015, https://www.womenshealthmag. com/beauty/a19910278/doves-choose-beautiful-campaign/.

26. Ibid.

Chapter 2: Girlhood Interrupted

1. "Sexualization of Girls Is Linked to Common Mental Health Problems in Girls and Women—Eating Disorders, Low Self-Esteem, and Depression," February 19, 2007, www.apa.org/releases/sexualization.aspx.

2. Ibid.

3. Cited in Ginny Olson, *Teenage Girls: Exploring Issues Adolescent Girls Face and Strategies to Help Them*, from A. E. Field et al., "Exposure to the Mass Media and Weight Concerns Among Girls," *Pediatrics* 103 (March 1999).

4. APA study; (Frederickson & Roberts, 1997; McKinley & Hyde, 1996).

5. C. S. Lewis, *The Last Battle* (New York: HarperCollins Publishers, 1956).

Chapter 3: Identity Crisis

1. Definition of gender fluid.

2. "Gen Z: The Culture, Beliefs and Motivations Shaping the Next Generation," Barna Group, January 23, 2018.

3. Ibid.

4. James Strong, S.T.D., LL.D., *A Concise Dictionary of the Words in the Greek Testament and The Hebrew Bible* (Bellingham, WA: Logos Research Systems, Inc., 2009), Vol. 1:58.

5. Douglas Wilson, *Reforming Marriage* (Moscow, ID: Canon Press, 2009), Kindle Edition, 80.

6. Douglas Wilson, *Federal Husband* (Moscow, ID: Canon Press, 1999), 27.

7. Douglas Wilson, *Fidelity* (Moscow, ID: Canon Press, 1999), Kindle Locations 978–985.

Chapter 4: Hooked on Screens

1. Jean M. Twenge, "Have Smartphones Destroyed a Generation?" (September 2017); https://www.theatlantic.com/magazine/archive/2017/09/has-the-smartphone-destroyed-a-generation/534198/.

2. Ibid.

3. Jean M. Twenge, PhD, *iGen: Why Today's Super-Connected Kids Are Growing Up Less Rebellious, More Tolerant, Less Happy—and Completely Unprepared for Adulthood—and What That Means for the Rest of Us* (New York: Atria Books, 2017).

4. Jean M. Twenge, "Have Smartphones Destroyed a Generation?" (September 2017); https://www.theatlantic.com/magazine/archive/2017/09/has-the-smartphone-destroyed-a-generation/534198/.

5. Ibid.

6. Twenge, *iGen*, 97.

7. Ibid.

8. Ibid., 98.

9. Ibid., 103–104.

10. Ibid.

11. Ibid., 108.

12. Nicholas Kardaras, *Glow Kids: How Screen Addiction Is Hijacking Our Kids—and How to Break the Trance* (New York: St. Martin's Griffin, 2017).

13. Ibid.

14. Ibid., 3.

15. Ibid., 59.

16. Ibid., 22.

17. "Facebook Is Addictive Because It 'Exploits a Vulnerability in People's Brains,'" cofounder Sean Parker says by Julia Glum on November 10, 2017, http://www.newsweek.com/russia-facebook-trump-sean-parker-707964.

18. Tony Reinke, *12 Ways Your Phone Is Changing You* (Wheaton, IL: Crossway: 2017).

19. Ibid., 44. Blaise Pascal, *Thoughts, Letters, and Minor Works*, ed. Charles W. Eliot, trans. W. F. Trotter, M. L. Booth, and O. W. Wight (New York: P.F. Collier & Son, 1910), 63.

Chapter 5: The Friendship Factor

1. Terri Apter, *You Don't Really Know Me: Why Mothers and Daughters Fight and How Both Can Win* (Boston, MA: W. W. Norton & Co., 2004), 33, cited in Ginny Olson, *Teenage Girls: Exploring Issues Adolescent Girls Face and Strategies to Help Them* (Grand Rapids, MI: Zondervan, 2006), 166.

2. Peter Bearman and Hannah Bruchner, et al, "Peer Potential: Making the Most of How Teens Influence Each Other," www.teenpregnancy.org, cited in Anita M. Smith, "The Power of Peers," www.youthdevelopment.org/articles/fp109901.htm.

3. Ibid.

4. Jean M. Twenge, PhD, *iGen: Why Today's Super-Connected Kids Are Growing Up Less Rebellious, More Tolerant, Less Happy—and Completely Unprepared for Adulthood—and What That Means for the Rest of Us* (New York: Atria Books, 2017), 57.

Chapter 6: Boy, Oh Boy

1. Suzannah Weiss, "Quarter of Young People Think Pressuring Someone Into Sex Is Normal," February 24, 2016, https://www.glamour.com/story/a-quarter-of-young-women-think.

2. Ibid.

3. Joan Jacobs Brumberg, *The Body Project* (New York: Random House, 1997), 11.

4. Francine Benton, *Etiquette: The Complete Guide for Day-to-Day Living the Correct Way* (New York: Random House, 1956).

5. Melissa Trevathan and Sissy Goff, *All You Need to Know about Raising Girls* (Grand Rapids, MI: Zondervan, 2007), 162.

6. Ibid.

Chapter 7: Beyond the Birds and Bees

1. "Then and Now," *Parents' Magazine* (January 1938).

2. *Hooked*, authors Joe S. McIlhaney, M.D., and Freda McKissic Bush, M.D., say, "Sex can be considered one of the appetites with which we are born."

3. Ibid.

4. Ibid.

5. Jean M. Twenge, PhD, *iGen: Why Today's Super-Connected Kids Are Growing Up Less Rebellious, More Tolerant, Less Happy—and Completely Unprepared for Adulthood—and What That Means for the Rest of Us* (New York: Atria Books, 2017), 205–206.

6. Ibid.

7. Joan Jacobs Brumberg, *The Body Project*, "Studies of risky behavior in adolescence reveal that boys and girls from all social classes experience a lag between the body's capability and the mind's capacity to comprehend the consequences of sex. In other words: adolescents are capable of reproduction, and they display sexual interest, before their minds are able to do the kind of reasoning necessary for the long-term, hypothetical planning that

sexuality requires (How would I care for a baby? What would we do if I became pregnant?)," 204.

8. Jane E. Brody, "Teenage Risks, and How to Avoid Them," December 18, 2007, www.nytimes.com/2007/12/18/health/18brod .html?pagewanted=1&_r=1&ref=science?_r=1.

9. Ibid.

10. In a study of 279 female adolescents published in the *Archives of Pediatrics and Adolescent Medicine* in June 2006, about 41 percent of girls ages fourteen to seventeen reported having "unwanted sex." Most of the girls had "unwanted sex because they feared the partner would get angry if denied sex."

11. National Campaign to Prevent Teen Pregnancy, 2004.

12. Dawn Eden, *The Thrill of the Chaste: Finding Fulfillment While Keeping Your Clothes On* (Nashville, TN: Thomas Nelson, 2006), 35.

13. Zahra Barnes, "This Is What Really Happens When You Wait Until Marriage to Have Sex"; https://www.self.com/story/waiting-until-marriage; October 4, 2016.

14. Youth Risk Behavior Surveillance—United States, 2015, https://www.cdc.gov/healthyyouth/data/yrbs/pdf/2015/ss6506_updated.pdf.

15. Hanna Rosin, "Even Evangelical Teens Do It: How Religious Beliefs Do and Don't Influence Sexual Behavior," May 30, 2007, www.slate.com/id/2167293, from Mark Regnerus, *Forbidden Fruit: Sex & Religion in the Lives of American Teenagers* (Oxford University Press, 2007). The book is a serious work of sociology based on several comprehensive surveys of young adults, coupled with in-depth interviews.

16. Ibid.

17. Diana Jean Schemo, "Mothers of Sex-Active Youths Often Think They're Virgins," the *New York Times*, www.nytimes.com/2002/09/05 /national/05SEX.html.

18. Hanna Rosin, "Even Evangelical Teens Do It: How Religious Beliefs Do and Don't Influence Sexual Behavior," May 30, 2007,

www.slate.com/id/2167293, from Mark Regnerus, *Forbidden Fruit: Sex & Religion in the Lives of American Teenagers* (Oxford University Press, 2007).

19. David Larson and Mary Ann Mayo, "Believe Well, Live Well," Family Research Council (1994).

20. David B. Larson, M.D., NMSPH, et al, "The Costly Consequences of Divorce: Assessing the Clinical, Economic, and Public Health Impact of Marital Disruption in the United States," National Institute for Healthcare Research, Rockville, Maryland, (1994): 84–85.

21. 1995 National Survey of Family Growth. National Center for Health Statistics. "Cycle 5: Public Use Date Files, Codebooks and Documentation," available at cdc.gov/nchs/about/major/nsfg/nsfg1-5doc_5.htm.

22. Wendy Shalit, "Girls Gone Mild, Data from National Longitudinal Study of Youth from 1979 to 2000." This study of more than seven thousand men and women (at age eighteen and again at age thirty-eight) found that individuals who were abstinent until marriage had only half the risk of divorce of nonabstinent. Couples who saved sex for their wedding night have a divorce rate three times lower than that of other couples, 64.

23. Sex education: Start discussions early, www.mayoclinic.com /health/sex-education/HQ00547.

24. See www.cnn.com/HEALTH.html.

25. Sex education: Start discussions early, www.mayoclinic.com /health/sex-education/HQ00547.

Chapter 8: Play Now, Pay Later

1. Jean M. Twenge, PHD, *iGen: Why Today's Super-Connected Kids Are Growing Up Less Rebellious, More Tolerant, Less Happy— and Completely Unprepared for Adulthood—and What That Means for the Rest of Us* (New York: Atria Books, 2017), 209.

2. Ibid.

3. *A Practical Guide to Culture: Helping the Next Generation Navigate Today's World*; Location 1824

4. Independent Women's Forum study "Hooking Up, Hanging Out, and Hoping for Mr. Right."

5. Ibid.

6. K. Christensson et al., "Effect of Nipple Stimulation on Uterine Activity and on Plasma Levels of Oxytocin in Full Term, Healthy, Pregnant Women," Acta Obstetricia et Gynecologica Scandinavia 68 (1989): 205–10; Larry J. Young and Zuoxin Wang, "The Neurobiology of Pair Bonding," Nature Neuroscience 7, no. 10 (October 2004): 1048–54; K. M. Kendrick, "Oxytocin, Motherhood, and Bonding," Experimental Physiology 85 (March 2000): 111S–124S, cited in "Unprotected: A Campus Psychiatrist Reveals How Political Correctness in Her Profession Endangers Every Student."

7. Anonymous, M.D, *Unprotected: A Campus Psychiatrist Reveals How Political Correctness in Her Profession Endangers Every Student.*

8. Michael Kosfeld, et al., "Oxytocin Increases Trust in Humans," Nature 435 (June 2005): 673.

9. http://www.reallifeanswers.org/family/marriage-preparation/the-benefits-of-chastity-before-marriage

10. Dawn Eden, *The Thrill of the Chaste: Finding Fulfillment While Keeping Your Clothes On* (Notre Dame, IN: Ave Maria Press, 2015), 32–33.

11. Wendy Shalit, "Girls Gone Mild, The National Longitudinal Survey of Adolescent Health," Wave II (1996).

12. Robert E. Rector, Kirk A. Johnson, and Lauren R. Noyes, "Sexually Active Teenagers Are More Likely to Be Depressed and to Attempt Suicide," Heritage Center for Data Analysis, 2003, www.heritage.org.

13. K. Joyner and R. Udry, "You Don't Bring Me Anything but Down: Adolescent Romance and Depression," *Journal of Health and Social Behavior* 41, no. 4 (December 2000): 369–91, cited in *Unprotected: A Campus Psychiatrist Reveals How Political Correctness*

in Her Profession Endangers Every Student, Anonymous, M.D. See also Deeanna Franklin, "Romantic Stress Tied to Depression in Sensitive Girls," *Clinical Psychiatric News*, April 2005, 31; and Denise D. Hallfors et al., "Which Comes First in Adolescence—Sex and Drugs or Depression?" *American Journal of Preventive Medicine* 29, no. 3 (2005): 163–70.

14. https://www.cdc.gov/std/products/youth-sti-infographic.pdf

15. Ibid.

16. https://www.cdc.gov/std/life-stages-populations/Youthand STDs-Dec-2017.pdf

17. https://www.cdc.gov/std/hpv/stdfact-hpv.htm

18. https://www.cdc.gov/std/chlamydia/default.htm

19. Anonymous, M.D., *Unprotected: A Campus Psychiatrist Reveals How Political Correctness in Her Profession Endangers Every Student*, 118.

20. Ibid., 110.

21. Maryann Leslie and Richard St. Pierre, "Osteoporosis: Implications for Risk Reduction in the College Setting," *Journal of American College Health* 48 (September 1999), 114–15.

22. Ibid., 115.

23. Krissy Brady, "Teen Pregnancy Statistics," May 4, 2016, https://www.teenvogue.com/story/teen-pregnancy-prevention-facts.

24. Planned Parenthood Report, "Pregnancy and Childbearing Among U.S. Teens"

25. Ibid.

26. https://www.cdc.gov/teenpregnancy/about/index.htm

27. http://www.candiesfoundation.org/theFacts

28. Teen Pregnancy Prevention; 3-12-2018; http://www.ncsl.org/research/health/teen-pregnancy-prevention.aspx.

29. Ibid.

30. Pregnancy Among US Teens; https://www.plannedparenthood.org/files/5714/0545/7055/Pregnancy_And_Childbearing_Among_US_Teens.pdf.

31. Teen Pregnancy Prevention; 3-12-2018; http://www.ncsl.org/research/health/teen-pregnancy-prevention.aspx.

32. National Campaign to Prevent Teen Pregnancy. "With One Voice 2004: America's Adults and Teens Sound Off about Teen Pregnancy" (December 2004).

33. Alan Guttmacher Institute website, www.agi-usa.org.

34. The Henry J. Kaiser Family Foundation, "Sexual Health of Adolescents and Young Adults in the United States."

35. Abortion Surveillance—United States, 2014Surveillance Summaries / November 24, 2017 / 66(24); 1–48, https://www.cdc.gov/mmwr/volumes/66/ss/ss6624a1.htm?s_cid=ss6624a1_w.

36. Alan Guttmacher Institute website, www.agi-usa.org.

Chapter 9: A New and Improved Sex Talk

1. Alan Guttmacher Institute.

2. The National Campaign to Prevent Teen Pregnancy.

3. Pam Stenzel with Crystal Kirgiss, *Sex Has a Price Tag: Discussions about Sexuality, Spirituality, and Self-Respect* (Grand Rapids, MI: Zondervan, 2003).

4. The National Campaign to Prevent Teen Pregnancy.

5. Neil Howe and William Strauss, *Millennials Rising: The Next Great Generation* (New York: Vintage Books, 200), 200.

6. Diana Jean Schemo, "Mothers of Sex-Active Youths Often Think They're Virgins," www.nytimes.com/2002/09/05/national/05SEX.html.

7. Ibid.

8. "Gen Z: The Culture, Beliefs and Motivations Shaping the Next Generation," Barna Group, January 23, 2018, 57.

9. https://www.cnn.com/2014/11/18/living/teens-sexting-what-parents-can-do/index.html; Sources original study: http://drexel.edu/now/archive/2014/June/Sexting-Study/

10. Ibid.

11. https://www.barna.com/research/porn-in-the-digital-age-new-research-reveals-10-trends/

12. Ibid.

13. Ibid.

14. Researchers at the University of New Hampshire found that about 90 percent of children between the ages of eight and sixteen have looked at porn. http://www.guardchild.com/statistics/.

15. https://www.barna.com/research/porn-in-the-digital-age-new-research-reveals-10-trends/

16. Mary Anne Layden, codirector of the Sexual Trauma and Psychopathology Program at the University of Pennsylvania's Center for Cognitive Therapy.

17. Gary Wilson, *Your Brain on Porn* (UK: Commonwealth Publishing, 2014), location 444; disclaimer: secular book and finding.

18. Albert Mohler, "Hijacking the Brain—How Pornography Works," *Christian Post* (February 3, 2010); https://www.christianpost.com/news/hijacking-the-brain-how-pornography-works-43600/.

Chapter 10: Forever Young

1. Jean M. Twenge, PhD, *iGen: Why Today's Super-Connected Kids Are Growing Up Less Rebellious, More Tolerant, Less Happy—and Completely Unprepared for Adulthood—and What That Means for the Rest of Us* (New York: Atria Books, 2017).

2. Ibid.

3. Ibid.

4. Ibid.

5. Ibid.

6. Ibid.

7. "Gen Z: The Culture, Beliefs and Motivations Shaping the Next Generation," Barna Group, January 23, 2018, 28; original source: David Kinnaman and Gabe Lyons, *Good Faith: Being a Christian When Society Thinks You're Irrelevant and Extreme.*

8. http://www.foxnews.com/us/2017/12/23/pennsylvania-family-ordered-to-take-down-jesus-christmas-display-after-neighbor-said-it-was-offensive.html

9. FoxNews.com article: http://www.foxnews.com/us/2016/11/17/coddling-campus-crybabies-students-take-up-toddler-therapy-after-trump-win.html.

10. Twenge, *iGen*, 164.

11. "Gen Z: The Culture, Beliefs and Motivations Shaping the Next Generation," Barna Group, January 23, 2018, 164.

12. Ibid., 34; original: https://www.theatlantic.com/magazine/archive/2014/04/hey-parents-leave-those-kids-alone/358631/.

13. "Gen Z: The Culture, Beliefs and Motivations Shaping the Next Generation, Barna Group, January 23, 2018, 35.

14. https://www.theatlantic.com/magazine/archive/2014/04/hey-parents-leave-those-kids-alone/358631/

15. "Gen Z: The Culture, Beliefs and Motivations Shaping the Next Generation," Barna Group, January 23, 2018, 52.

16. Ibid.

Chapter 11: Ready, Set, Launch!

1. Leonard Sax, M.D., PhD, *Boys Adrift* (New York: Basic Books, 2009), 142–43.

2. *Time* magazine article entitled "Grow Up? Not So Fast;" By Lev Grossman Sunday, Jan. 16, 2005; http://content.time.com/time/magazine/article/0,9171,1018089,00.html.

Chapter 12: It's Okay to Dream about Marriage and Motherhood

1. https://i.redd.it/qn25qiv8fawz.png

2. http://www.chicagotribune.com/lifestyles/ct-marriage-in-decline-balancing-20150518-column.html

3. https://census.gov/data/tables/time-series/demo/families/marital.html

4. Jean M. Twenge, PhD, *iGen: Why Today's Super-Connected Kids Are Growing Up Less Rebellious, More Tolerant, Less Happy—and*

Completely Unprepared for Adulthood—and What That Means for the Rest of Us (New York: Atria Books, 2017), 219.

5. Ibid., 220.

6. "Gen Z: The Culture, Beliefs and Motivations Shaping the Next Generation," Barna Group, January 23, 2018, 53.

7. Albert Mohler, "The Case Against Marriage," Newsweek, http://www.albertmohler.com/2010/06/25/the-case-against-marriage -courtesy-of-newsweek, posted on June 25, 2010.

8. http://www.foxnews.com/lifestyle/2017/09/02/cheap-sex-is -making-men-give-up-on-marriage-author-says.html

9. Ibid.

10. Segelstein, "Late Dates: The Dangerous Art of Marital Procrastination"; www.salvomag.com/new/articles/salvo8/8segelstein .php.

11. Ibid.

12. Frederica Mathewes-Green, essay in "First Things," August/ September 2005, http://www.firstthings.com, as cited in Albert Mohler, "What If There Are No Adults?"; https://www.chris-tianheadlines.com/columnists/al-mohler/what-if-there-are-no-adults-1413383.html, posted on August 19, 2005.

13. Ibid.

14. Jessica Bennett and Jesse Ellison, "The Case against Marriage," Newsweek, June 11, 2010, https://www.newsweek.com/ cse-against-marriage-73045.

15. Wendy Shalit, *Girls Gone Mild: Young Women Reclaim Self-Respect and Find It's Not Bad to Be Good* (New York: Random House, 2007), 19.

16. *Sex without Strings, Relationships without Rings: Today's Young Singles Talk about Mating and Dating*, A Publication of the National Marriage Project © 2000, www.marriage.rutgers.edu.

17. Pamela Smock, a family demographer at the University of Michigan, says about 70 percent of those who get married lived together first. "Cohabitation is continuing to grow, and it's become the model way of life."

18. *Sex without Strings, Relationships Without Rings: Today's Young Singles Talk about Mating and Dating.*

19. The National Marriage Project's Ten Things to Know Series, "The Top Ten Myths of Marriage" (March 2002); Alfred DeMaris and K. Vaninadha Rao, "Premarital Cohabitation and Marital Instability in the United States: A Reassessment," *Journal of Marriage and the Family* 54 (1992): 178–90.

20. Naomi Schaefer, "How Shacking Up Leads to Divorce," February 9, 2015, https://nypost.com/2015/02/09/how-shacking-up-leads-to-divorce/.

21. "Sociological Reasons Not to Live Together from All about Cohabiting Before Marriage," http://www.leaderu.com/critical/cohabitation-socio.html.

22. Linda J. Waite and Kara Joyner, "Emotional and Physical Satisfaction with Sex in Married, Cohabitating, and Dating Sexual Unions: So Men and Women Differ?" 239–69 in E. O. Laumann and R. T. Michael, eds., *Sex, Love, and Health in America* (Chicago, IL: University of Chicago Press, 2001); Edward O. Laumann, J. H. Gagnon, R. T. Michael and S. Michaels, *The Social Organization of Sexuality: Sexual Practices in the United States* (Chicago, IL: University of Chicago Press, 1994).

23. Twenge, *iGen*, 218.

24. Ibid., Shalit, *Girls Gone Mild.* "Marital Status and health: US 1999–2002," Report from Centers for Disease Control (2004). This study, based on interviews with 127,545 adults age eighteen-plus, found that married adults were in better psychological and physical health than cohabiting, single, or divorced adults.

25. *Sex without Strings, Relationships without Rings.*

26. Ibid.

27. Ibid.

28. Ibid.

29. Marcia Segelstein, "Late Dates: The Dangerous Art of Marital Procrastination," *Salvo*, Issue 8 (Spring 2009), www.salvo-mag.com.

30. Wendy Shalit, *Girls Gone Mild: Young Women Reclaim Self-Respect and Find It's Not Bad to Be Good* (New York: Random House, 2007), 4.

31. Ibid.

32. Albert Mohler, "So There Are Limits After All," June 6, 2007, www.bpnews.net/25848/.

33. Zev Rosenwaks, "We Still Can't Stop the Biological Clock," *New York Times*, June 24, 2000.

34. Sylvia Hewlett, *Creating a Life: Professional Women and the Quest for Children* (New York, 2002), 217.

35. *American Society for Reproductive Medicine, Age and Fertility, a Guide for Patients* (Birmingham, AL: American Society for Reproductive Medicine, 2003), 3.

36. Hewlett, *Creating a Life*, 219.

37. Kate Johnson, "Oocyte Freezing: Insurance or False Security?" Clinical Psychiatry News, February 2005, 76.

38. *American Society for Reproductive Medicine, American Society for Reproductive Medicine Guide for Patients, Infertility: An Overview*, 4.

39. Ibid.

40. A. D. Domar et al., "The Psychological Impact of Infertility: A Comparison with Patients with Other Medical Conditions," *Journal of Psychosomatic Obstetrics and Gynecology* 14 suppl. (1993): 45–52.

Chapter 13: Who Can Find a Virtuous Woman?

1. VW book; Jamieson-Fausset-Brown Bible Commentary.

2. *The Holman Illustrated Bible Dictionary* (Nashville, B&H Publishing Group, 2003).

3. Merrill F. Unger, *The New Unger's Bible Dictionary* (Chicago: Moody, 2006).

Chapter 14: Grounded for Life

1. LifeWay Study.

2. Jossey-Bass Study, San Francisco, 2009.

3. America's Changing Religious Landscape Study (Pew Research Center).

4. Christian Smith and Melinda Lundquist Denton, *Soul Searching: The Religious and Spiritual Lives of American Teenagers* (Oxford University Press, 2005).

5. "Gen Z: The Culture, Beliefs and Motivations Shaping the Next Generation," Barna Group, January 23, 2018, 97.

6. Ibid.

7. Ibid., 82.

8. Ibid., 88.

9. *Ladies' Home Journal* (December 1948), 185.

10. J. I. Packer, *Knowing God* (Downers Grove, IL: InterVarsity Press, 1973), 19.

Appendix

1. "Kids and Screen Time: Signs Your Child Might Be Addicted," December 1, 2017, https://news.umich.edu/kids-and-screen-time-signs-your-child-might-be-addicted/.

2. Ibid.

3. https://www.cdc.gov/std/life-stages-populations/Youthand STDs-Dec-2017.pdf.

4. Krissy Brady, "13 Facts about Teen Pregnancy That Will Blow Your Mind," (MAY 4, 2016), https://www.teenvogue.com/story/teen-pregnancy-prevention-facts.

5. The Candie's Foundation

6. Planned Parenthood Report, "Pregnancy and Childbearing Among U.S. Teens."

7. The Candies Foundation

8. U.S. Department of Health & Human Services, Office on Adolescent Health, "Trends in Teen Pregnancy and Childbearing."

9. Planned Parenthood Report, "Pregnancy and Childbearing Among U.S. Teens."

10. National Conference of State Legislatures, "Teen Pregnancy Prevention."

11. Ibid.

12. Planned Parenthood Report, "Pregnancy and Childbearing Among U.S. Teens."

13. Ibid.

14. National Conference of State Legislatures, "Teen Pregnancy Prevention."

15. The Henry J. Kaiser Family Foundation, "Sexual Health of Adolescents and Young Adults in the United States."

16. JAMA Pediatrics; February 26, 2018. doi:10.1001/jamapediatrics.2017.5745

17. https://www.womenshealth.gov/relationships-and-safety/sexual-assault-and-rape/sexual-assault

Also Available

BY VICKI COURTNEY

for mothers & daughters

for tweens

for teens

Also Available

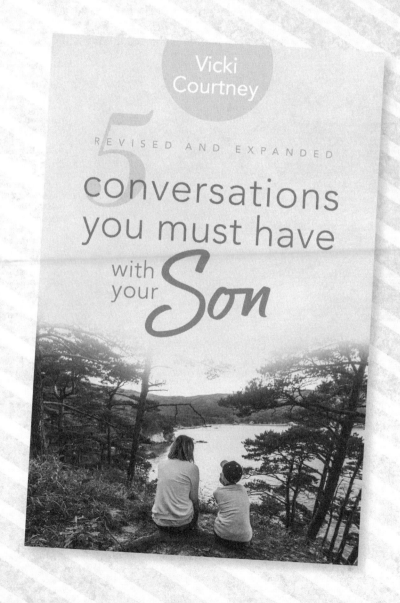

Vicki Courtney

REVISED AND EXPANDED

5 conversations you must have with your Son